DICKS!

GO, JANE!

Other Works by Allie Chee

NEW MOTHER
Using a Doula, Midwife, Postpartum Doula, Maid, Cook, or Nanny to Support Healing, Bonding and Growth

FREE LOVE
Everyday Ideas for Joyful Living

GO, JANE!

Ancient Wisdom and
Modern Street Smarts for
Dealing with Dicks

ALLIE CHEE

HESTIA
BOOKS & MEDIA

Disclaimer: This book is intended for information purposes only. The approaches, techniques, and services described herein are meant to supplement, and not to be a substitute for, professional medical care or treatment. They should not be used to treat any ailment or concern without prior consultation with a qualified health care professional. This book is not intended as a replacement for such guidance nor may the author or publisher be found responsible for any adverse effects resulting from the use of information in this book.

No part of this publication may be reproduced or transmitted in any form or by any means, electronic, digital, or mechanical, including photocopy, recording, or any information storage or retrieval system, without the express prior written permission of the publisher, except in the case of brief quotations embodied in critical reviews and certain other non-commercial uses permitted by copyright law.

Published in the United States by
Hestia Books & Media
1111 West El Camino Real, #109-207
Sunnyvale, CA 94087

Copyright © 2013 by Allie Chee. All rights reserved under International and Pan-American Copyright Conventions.

ISBN 10: 0985626445
EAN 13: 9780985626440
First Hestia Books & Media edition 2013.
Editorial team: David Colin Carr, Karen Murphy
Cover design by Laura Coyle

For more information about Allie Chee and her work, visit:

Web: www.alliechee.com
Blog: www.gojanebook.blogspot.com

Printed in the United States of America on FSC-certified, 30% post consumer recycled paper.

I give it to them loud and dirty, so they won't forget it.

–GENERAL GEORGE S. PATTON

Dear Reader,

I started writing *Go, Jane!* in 2007, and completed Part 1: *Run, Jane!* in 2008. That was when I was still single—and fresh out of a brush with a Dick. If I'd finished it then, I would have dedicated it to my sisters—about a billion women on Earth.

It's 2012 at the time of writing this dedication, I'm a married woman with a two-year-old daughter, and I've just completed Part 2: *Love, Jane!* Since I'm now writing as a mother, I would dedicate the work to all my *daughters*—about a billion women on Earth.

When I first started writing, I thought my readers would be the 18-25 group. But as more and more women read the manuscript, I discovered women of all ages need to learn—or be reminded of—these lessons. An 83-year-old woman, after reading one particular section, said, "I just had something similar happen last week. I wish I'd read *Go, Jane!* a month ago!" So, it's also dedicated to all my mothers on Earth—about a billion women, which brings our grand total to about 3 billion women!

You'll find the tones of the two main parts of the work are different.

Any woman who finds herself in any of the situations in Part 1 needs to be shaken, needs tough love, needs someone to help guide her out of the mess she's in! Part 1: *Run, Jane!* isn't loud and dirty, but it's *frank* and leaves little to question. And I hope you won't forget it.

The voice in Part 2 isn't wimpy, but it's a strong, loving embrace rather than a kick in the pants.

Both voices have their place in sharing and learning, and I hope you find meaning and benefit in both.

With love, *damn it!*

Allie

P.S. As you read, please try to keep in mind the ancient Luyia proverb of Western Kenya:

A messenger cannot be beaten.

CONTENTS

Introduction: Who is Jane? Who is Dick? Who Cares? xiii

Part 1: Run, Jane!

Chapter 1: What Our Mothers Didn't Tell Us
(and why they didn't) 1

Chapter 2: Predator and Prey 9

Chapter 3: How to Spot Stranger Dick 13

Chapter 4: The Dick You Know 33

Chapter 5: The Worst Dick of All: Family Dick 97

Part 2: Love, Jane!

Chapter 6: Beyond Predator and Prey 149

Chapter 7: Chill, Jane! 157

Chapter 8: Being Your Own Best Friend 163

Chapter 9: Special Chapter on Internet Dating 185

Chapter 10: Your Thing 197

Chapter 11: Do a Man-Fast 201

INTRODUCTION

WHO IS JANE? WHO IS DICK? WHO CARES?

It was not until my conversation with Mother Teresa in 1993[1], over a scratchy phone connection between Laguna Beach and Calcutta, that I began to seriously contemplate the meaning of self-love and its implication in the events in my life. But as we'll see in the coming pages, self-love (or lack thereof) is a great determining factor in how we deal with, overcome encounters with and learn to avoid Dicks.

It is the nature of human beings to neglect the subjects of self-love, facing down demons, and finding true peace and tranquility—until their hearts are broken, they're financially broke or life pulls the rug out from under them. Peace and tranquility bring happiness, but that will remain elusive as long as we're unaware that the activities and thoughts in which we engage are in direct opposition to that goal.

---

1 More on this conversation in Part 2.

Many of us run through our lives like the poor hamster, ever faster and increasingly exhausted, thinking we're pursuing what makes us happy. But through ignorance, we're running as fast as we can in the direction of emotional excess, loss and pain.

Why ever would we do that? Simply because we don't know that's where we're headed—or we know but can't stop ourselves.

Therefore, one approach to finding happiness is to look at the ridiculous things we're doing that are creating loads of unhappiness. Then we need to STOP IT long enough to reflect on creating true peace and tranquility—before life stops us in an ugly way.

To be clear, this is not a book about achieving happiness. That is a pursuit that transcends relationships with other people. It is, rather, about understanding and managing relationships in a better way to support health and harmony in our pursuit of happiness and meaning in life.

My fingers are usually used to cook, clean, type and cultivate my garden. However, in this book and with this subject, they have another use—especially that middle one. And I use it in the following pages. As a friend of mine from Jamaica says, "Sometime, Allie, der's no-ting to do but *give 'em da finga!*"

We are living—for now—on the physical plane. And the reality is that the life cycle on Earth involves a prey-and-predator phenomenon. When people (women, in the case of my audience) don't rise above it, they fall victim to it. I've written this book in the hope that my fellow sisters can either avoid altogether situations in which they are "victims" or "prey"—or if they find their likeness in these stories, they can learn how to knock it off and live with more peace and joy.

Who is Jane?

There are three types of women in the world, generally speaking.

The first group is intact—meaning *generally* stable, and mentally and spiritually healthy. They know what they want from life, what they have to give and they go for it. Of course they have issues, but they manage and work to improve them.

What are their issues? Perhaps, among others, these women during the course of their lives were caught off guard and ill prepared when they've crossed paths with a Dick. They were robbed of their innocence, and set back emotionally, physically, spirituality and/or financially by the experience; but they are willing to exert the energy to move forward.

Be warned: Not all women in this category are highly noble and intelligent creatures. Many are misguided, naïve and lack moral integrity, or are bubbleheads, dizzy and cheap. You'll be learning about them in the following pages. The good news is, most of them are not beyond help. They can recover themselves and improve their lives, starting here on these pages. Those who are truly hopeless go into another category.

The second group of women, like group one, is also "Jane," the difference being that they have yet to be injured in any way by a Dick. For the few in this group already old enough to read, this book will serve to prepare these women for the inevitable encounter by which they'll otherwise be blindsided. In addition to reading this book, these Janes ought to start a support group like the living survivors of World War II. They'll have about the same number of members.[2]

Finally, there is the third group of women—for whom we have as much fondness as we do for Dicks. This group is *not* Jane. For whatever unfortunate reason, they've slipped off the street of sanity into the pothole of living hell and, rather than doing the work to recover their way, they use their energy to pull others down in their hellhole with them.

---

[2] This is, naturally, intended to demonstrate a truth with humor. You'll discover in the coming pages that it is not in any way a condemnation of men in general, and is simply an honest acknowledgement of the hazards of life on the planet. If you've seen *National Geographic,* you know what I'm talking about.

You can recognize one easily by knowing the behavioral clues to look for.

The classic: incessant gossiping, gold-digging, blame-laying, backstabbing, using sex and their paycheck progeny as weapons. That's a brief list of the most nefarious.

The new ones: conducting endless searches online for "dirt" on her every acquaintance, but especially on her exes, her exes' exes and her exes' currents; strange and inappropriate posts on their multiple social website pages, which are full of hundreds of "friends" few of whom would even loan her a five-spot; and a long list of other activities that make the civilized person in her path want to flee to a remote island.

This kind of woman doles out destruction on any poor sap in her path, male or female—and blames others for her self-inflicted misery. In short, this character is a she-Dick.

This book is not intended for this third group of women. There are many other books intended for she-Dicks that we all hope they read (though they will likely never crack the cover of any).

Who is Dick?

This subject will be discussed at length, so to speak. In the meantime, we'll define him thus: the creep or criminal who attempts to spread his negativity on the lives of others.

"If you prick us, do we not bleed?
–WILLIAM SHAKESPEARE

Who Cares?

Back to Jane. Why would anyone care about her predator-and-prey survival training—or lack thereof?

Any well-trained and strong animal can cruise through life relatively unscathed by their predators. The weak and those with compromised or no training are the pitiful puffs of remaining fur we do not want to see skittering across the *Nature Channel*.

Most women are improperly trained to navigate the dangers they will encounter in their lifetimes. May this book serve as their rough guide to surviving the Dicks. Better trained women make happier, healthier women—who make happier wives, mothers, employees, friends and neighbors. Thus, everyone should care (except the small minority of Dicks and she-Dicks excluded by self-inflicted default…but we're praying for them).

PART 1

CHAPTER 1

WHAT OUR MOTHERS DIDN'T TELL US (AND WHY THEY DIDN'T)

By three methods we may learn wisdom: first, by reflection, which is the noblest; second, by imitation, which is the easiest; and third, by experience, which is the most bitter.

–CONFUCIUS

We need to make one thing clear: no man-haters here. Sincere, positive, loving women of the world, collectively "the Janes," love most of the men in their lives. We're crazy about men. *We love them in all shapes, colors and sizes!*

It's the sleazy, the creepy and the criminals—those who can be defined as "energy sumps"—that we'll call collectively "the Dicks," whom we could do without but must inevitably confront throughout our lives. These include their female counterparts, the she-Dicks, who merit their own time and place.

Why do we need a guidebook to surviving the Dicks when we should have learned this important survival information from our mothers and our tribe? Most mothers and animal groups in nature, besides loving, feeding and playing with their offspring, *teach* them how to survive and thrive in life. Specifically on the survival front, the mothers teach their offspring about their species' primary predators and how best to identify, avoid and give them the slip if an attack is in progress.

Many human mothers are like these caring, loving creatures. And when they are, the results can be astounding. Quick! Think of three of the most famous presidents of the United States. Did you say George Washington, Abraham Lincoln and Barrack Obama? Well, look at what these men had to say about the women who raised them.

*All that I am or ever hope to be,
I owe to my angel mother.*
–**ABRAHAM LINCOLN**

*All I am I owe to my mother. I attribute all my success
in life to the moral, intellectual and physical
education I received from her.*
–**GEORGE WASHINGTON**

[My grandmother] made me the man I am today.
–**BARACK OBAMA**

However, modern American society (and, increasingly so, every other nation) has made the formidable job of parents virtually impossible to pull off successfully in any area, much less all areas. How can a single or even two parents be everything?

Shop for and prepare real[3] food three times every day; educate, expose to art, culture and sport; impart wisdom; provide a safe, clean home; share fun and entertainment—all while working full time and maintaining personal health and peace. Impossible. A daunting inventory of all the results of the current approach to family life in the U.S. is unnecessary since:

a) it is witnessed daily on the telly and in the grocery and/or

b) it's *grim*.

But just a quick peek behind the curtain reveals that the world's greatest and most powerful wizard (nation) has a few issues with current familial and societal structures. Despite spending more money than any nation to prevent it, we are hugely obese, drugged

---

3   Here's a brief introduction to not-real, faux foodstuffs: anything passed through a car window and cast to kids in the back seat, goo out of freezer bags; nondescript, unidentifiable fried blobs; microwaved chemical logs (even if "certified organic"); anything with garish, frightening clowns on the front or plastic landfill-bound toys inside; anything with numbers in the ingredient list, e.g., Red #40; almost anything with an ingredient list longer than three items; and everything with words you can't pronounce in the ingredient list.

and broken. (We're lots of wonderful things too, but those don't need improvement, so they're not the subject here.)

Obviously, simply throwing money at issues doesn't work. Does anyone not on the receiving end of that money think it will? We're a rich society, but we're still in what is an altered version of survival mode. We are "surviving," but how many things slip through the cracks? The "little" things like: peace, health and happiness. And other things like: enjoying family and personal time.

Thus, in the face of these multifaceted and almost insurmountable challenges, many of our mothers and our tribe as a whole have forgotten to teach us about our greatest predator: Dicks.

Those who have not lived in other cultures may struggle with this concept, due to lack of perspective. Having trotted the globe at a furious pace for 20 years, I can say with plenty of earth to stand on that, while the U.S. excels in many areas and is a country I love and respect, family life here sucks the big one.

If you require further evidence and have the means, travel far and wide. If money's tight, you can simply repeat an experiment I've conducted in cabs all over the country. See following page.

Allie Chee's Anthropological Survey of Cab Drivers ®

Me: Hey, where are you from?

Driver: _____ (Fill in the blank with a country you consider wretched and is on government "don't visit" warning lists.)

Me: Do you miss it?

Driver: Oh, yes.

Me: Do you wish you could go back?

Driver: Yes.

Me: Why?

Driver: Choose one or more: a.) the life b.) the family c.) the culture d.) the beauty e.) the food.

Me: So why don't you go back?

Driver: Can't make any money there.

Me: Why?

Driver: Circle correct answer (hint, could be more than one): a) It's a desert. b) It's a jungle. c) It's war-torn. d) A hurricane flattened it. e) An earthquake turned it to rubble.

Me: So you stay here just for the money—to put food on the table?

Driver: Yep. That's the only reason.

So we've got Wild West entrepreneurialism, consumption-driven capitalism and tech-driven innovation down pat (or at least we thought we did. At the time of writing, even that's not been going so smoothly—but here's to it getting back on track).

Margaret Mead, who hasn't even witnessed what's transpired in the last 30 years (she's probably *quaking* in her grave), said it succinctly: "Nobody has ever before asked the nuclear family to live all by itself in a box the way we do. With no relatives, no support, we've been put in an impossible situation."

That's really grim, but what happens to those pitiful souls who don't even have that nuclear family?

That's just where we currently find ourselves. Just like Rita Mae Brown said, "*If the world were a logical place, men would ride side-saddle.*" It's clearly not. Our lives are filled not only with beautiful people and events, but also with illogical, violent and tragic experiences and contradictions. So how do we understand and move beyond it? How do we survive and rise above? If we weren't taught, we can give in to it, wallow and endure a life of drudgery, or we can get off our asses and teach ourselves. We can grow and change.

Now back to the jungle.

CHAPTER 2

PREDATOR AND PREY

Every morning in Africa, a gazelle wakes up. It knows it must outrun the fastest lion or it will be killed. Every morning in Africa, a lion wakes up. It knows it must run faster than the slowest gazelle, or it will starve. It doesn't matter whether you're the lion or a gazelle—when the sun comes up, you'd better be running.

–CHRISTOPHER MCDOUGALL

What is a gazelle's most likely predator? A lion. So what does its mother and the herd teach it to do, even if simply by their lead, when they sense the presence of a lion? Run! What is the seal's most likely predator? A shark. So what does its mother and the herd teach it to do when a shark shows up? Swim! What is a woman's most likely predator? A Dick.

Have you ever had a skirmish with a Dick? Surely. It happens all the time.

Have you ever been clotheslined—I mean caught completely off guard, tossed on your head and pummeled in the dirt—by a Dick? How long did it take you to shake it off and stand up—or did they have to take you away on a stretcher?

How could that have happened? Why didn't you see the attack coming and how come it was so difficult to recover?

Your training, or lack thereof.

What do women learn to do all too often from their mothers and society when approached or ensnared by a Dick?

- You're not that pretty (take what you can get).
- You don't want to lose your job (accept it).
- Be quiet (you don't want to cause trouble).
- It's your duty (you can't leave).
- Pretend like it isn't happening (meanwhile more and more people are negatively affected).
- Work it out (give him a sixth chance).
- Look the other way—especially if he is _____(fill in the blank with one or more: good-looking, rich, the right religion, from the right family, popular, powerful).

- If you have kids with him, you have to stay for the kids (it's your fault anyway).

Many of our mothers could hardly talk about men and menses in the same sentence without being nervous, so it's predictably unlikely they would figure out how to approach the subject of Dicks. Further, they are often children of, married to, dating or working for Dicks, so they do not even themselves know how to avoid and overcome the Dicks. Thus, patterns of abuse pass from mother to daughter until someone in the sad, broken line—against the odds—figures it out on their own and becomes the miracle story.

There are a few mothers in nature who, similarly, offer little or no training. The sea turtle, for example, crawls out of the ocean, painstakingly digs a hole in the sand, offloads her 100-200 little turtle eggs, buries them and then heads out to sea, never to be seen again.

Harsh!

The forsaken reptiles crack out of their shells only to be greeted by a host of prey that includes birds, raccoons, ghost crabs and, for the remainder who make it to the water, schools of hungry fish with a taste for young turtle. Only 10%[4] of hatchlings make it.

---

4   http://www.seaworld.org/infobooks/SeaTurtle/stlongevity.html, 3/3/9

Sadly, the number of women who successfully avoid attack by their predators rivals those of the turtle.

There are women who take the training of their young girls quite seriously. My friend Nancy from Kenya told me how her mother explained things to her when she was twelve: *Girl, you never sit with your legs open and your privates showing. Never! If you sit with your legs open in front of any man, even your father, his dick will go up in the air.*

I don't know about you, but growing up in Texas, our mothers *most certainly* didn't tell us that.

For those of you whose mothers went out to sea, leaving you vulnerable, or for those whose loving mother's direction fell short of Nancy's picturesque guidance, your training begins right now.

CHAPTER 3

HOW TO SPOT STRANGER DICK

The best armor is to keep out of range.

–ITALIAN PROVERB

Central to the Chinese concept of cosmic order is the idea that how things begin is indicative of how they will develop and end. Look at your own life and that of people around you, and ask yourself if this principle is applicable to relationships.

It is not always easy to identity which relationships will prove positive experiences long-term, but it is frighteningly obvious, with a trained and disciplined eye, which ones have no hope of a positive outcome. Therefore, since it is easy to predict which ones will have absurd endings, many heartbreaks and much wasted energy can be spared.

This and the following chapters include tips and colorful stories to illustrate the point and to teach you how to identify a Dick. Some of them are hypothetical situations in which you might find yourself. Others are events I've heard carried on the wind over the years (with all the details changed and stories mixed up and combined to protect the cast of characters). The men in these stories all offered telltale signs that they are Dicks. Do any of them have redeeming qualities or deserve a break from the harsh critique? Perhaps a few.

However, mixing it up with these characters and people like them is sure to bring frustration, hurt and scattered energy. We wish them well—sitting at home alone, perhaps reflecting on the supreme Dickiness of their ways, with us safely across town or continents. Read these stories and see in how many you can see your friends, your mother, your sister, your neighbor… yourself.

We've all lived these stories in varied ways.

The first category of Dick is Stranger Dick, meaning a man you do not yet know. Stranger Dick is lurking around every corner but is often easy to recognize and avoid. Our first examples from this category:

Hangin'-Around Dick

These are situations women encounter everyday, everywhere around the world, that often lead to nothing yet can and frequently do lead to trouble.

Jane is on a bus, in a café, at the library, sitting on a park bench, walking on a sidewalk—and a man she doesn't know sits down or walks right next to her.

If there is plenty of seating available—or *any* seating in the near vicinity—yet he chooses a seat right next to Jane (or to walk right next to or behind her on an otherwise empty sidewalk), the wise thing to do is to assume there is indeed a reason he chose to do that. And, there is only one of two reasons:

- He feels a little chemistry and would like to see if there's a possibility to chat (but has weak skills and little understanding of more appropriate ways to interact with and approach women he doesn't know)
- or he's a Dick with ill intentions.

To respond in the safest way we must assume that a stranger forcing himself next to us when it's unnecessary (again, if he had an immediate choice of other places) is aggressive—*at best.*

What to do in this situation?

If Jane feels a little chemistry and would like to chat, that's a choice but it must be pursued carefully—this is a total stranger (and looking friendly or "hot" does not change stranger status). Stay on guard.

If you feel even the slightest discomfort—do not stay where you are. Move *immediately.*

A few stories to illustrate:

Jane was sitting in a subway car that was almost empty. A man entered at the next stop and though there were 25 seats to choose from, he sat right across from her—staring.

Jane stood up and moved to the front of the car, putting as much space as possible between them. If this man had honest intentions, he might have recognized that he'd put her in an uncomfortable situation and would stop staring.

But what did this guy do?

He yelled with a glare and drunken slur, *"Do I scare you?"*

Yes, indeed—a Dick!

Jane's instincts were correct, and moving put invaluable space between her and what could be an attacker.

In our next example, Jane was traveling alone in a foreign country; she enjoyed meeting new people; and she spent her mornings walking the sidewalks and watching the morning bustle in the cafes in each town.

One quiet morning, she saw a man walking in her direction, but on the opposite side of the street. Then, he crossed in the middle of the street and began walking straight toward her with a big smile.

He seemed friendly enough and, wanting to be friendly in return, she smiled back.

Just as he passed her, he grabbed her wrist.

But this Jane—though friendly and a little slow on the draw this bright morning—was versed on the subject and knew how to respond.

"What the FUCK do you think you're doing? GET AWAY FROM ME!" she yelled as she yanked her arm back and ran away.

Taken aback by the force of her response, he went on his way—likely to look for a more docile target.

Lesson

This seems so simple—but we can't underestimate the importance of learning how to respond in this situation.

Again, if Jane feels comfortable, it's her choice to remain where she is and to engage with the stranger.

If for any reason and to any degree she feels uncomfortable, she should move immediately—and if possible—to a place with more people.

This dialogue is necessary because—as mentioned above—millions of women everyday are in similar situations, they feel uncomfortable, *but they don't move.*

When Jane is fortunate, her inability to move doesn't come with a price. But when it does, the price can be a mugging, being flashed, worse, or *far worse.*

Why do women, when they feel uncomfortable and want to move, fail to move? Ultimately it's what've we've already mentioned—lack of training. Specifically, it's out of fear of "appearing rude," "hurting someone's feelings," or "not wanting to start trouble." However, a Dick in this situation can definitely sense when a woman is uncomfortable, and her failure to respond is an indication of easy prey.

The lesson here is simple, easy, and can help prevent trouble in countless instances. When uncomfortable: Don't ponder. Don't question yourself. Don't dally. *Haul ass, Jane!*

Now on to our next characters in the tales of Stranger Dick…

Peacock Dick

You are sitting in a bar chatting with friends and suddenly a smoking-hot guy walks in with his equally attractive date. Conversation stops and reproductive hormones are released.

He is wearing ripped jeans and a black wife-beater with the name of his gym on the back. His hair says, "We just had great sex," and his shades say, "You can't see me, but I see you looking."

You don't notice many details of his date's attire because you are busy wondering how her precariously mounted torpedoes haven't launched from her tank top.

Later—since you've been staring—you notice that his date has gone to the bathroom. He looks over and sees you. You're embarrassed for being caught looking (but only a little), and to your surprise he gives you a big, sexy smile. Before the poor bubblehead finishes touching up her lipstick, rearranging her weapons and getting back to the table, this Dick's already strutted over to your table and given you his card (Personal Fitness Trainer).

Lesson

Jane, get a grip.

No, not on *him!* On yourself.

Throw away the card. If you decide to call him, you should write the date on your calendar, because within only a few weeks or months, you'll be the silly slob in the bathroom while he's giving his card to someone else. Then you'll be able to refer back to that calendar to see if Allie Chee was right when advising that it would take eight weeks or less to reveal that you hooked up with a Dick.

A peacock has too little in its head, and too much in its tail.
  –SWEDISH PROVERB

Premature Dick

You're shopping in your local organic grocery store, when *bam!* Right there in the nuts aisle is your dream man—and he's not wearing a wedding ring! You reach for the sunflower seeds and your hands accidentally touch—he eats sunflower seeds, too! You strike up a conversation and he gives you his card—a teacher at the local yoga studio. After a few classes and help with some special poses, he informs you that he's divorced.

Oh, wait—you can't come over to his house, because in fact he's not officially divorced yet. It was supposed to be done months and months ago, and well, the lawyers just keep dragging it out, you know how they are, and the ex can't ever agree on anything and nevertheless it's really, really over next month.

Lesson

Jane, for god's sake, please pull your head out. Think back to the last time you were fresh out of a serious relationship. Though you weren't aware of it at the time, weren't you reeling, weren't you wasting time (aka dating the guy from the drive-through window at Jack-in-the-Box because he looked cute and over 21; hooking up with long-time exes; or hoping you weren't contracting STDs), and didn't you truly need time *alone* to heal and regroup? So does he!

Run, Jane! Leave him alone. He may genuinely care for you and maybe you would make a good couple. But not now. For at least the next 12 months, this man cannot help but be a Dick. He needs time. Tell him to get that glorious and probably well-deserved ticket to freedom, wait at least a year, better two, and then call you for lunch. If it is meant to be, it will be there when he is divorced and healed.

The divorced person is like a man with a black patch over one eye. He looks rather dashing but the fact is that he has been through a maiming experience.

–JO COUDERT

And our last example of Stranger Dick…

Big Shot Dick

We usually don't expect men 6'5," 5% body fat, handsome *and* with a great voice to be shy, but it happens. Despite his phenomenal appearance and talent, he's been rather awkward with women and had few girlfriends. On his behalf, fate intervened.

His first track became a number one hit single and now it doesn't matter if he doesn't know how to make an approach; women flock to him. (I think it's really because of his efforts to reduce CO_2 emissions in the atmosphere and his campaign to eliminate illiteracy.)

Being new to the scene and exceptionally good looking, the tabloids found a moneymaker in him and were relentless. He loved it (even though he'd feel nauseous and couldn't eat for hours after a run-in); the ladies loved it; his producer loved it; and Jane, who had a secret connection, loved it.

Her connection was her friend Chrissy, the hairdresser for his brother's personal assistant. It was several degrees of separation, but it was close enough. Wherever Dick went, his brother went, and his brother's personal assistant blabbed to the hairdresser, and Chrissy texted Jane the moment she had foil in the assistant's hair!

"2nite flyguy club @ 11:00"
" :) c u there!" Jane texted back.

Jane wasn't going to let this chance pass. *I don't care how many chicks are in that club; he's going to notice me tonight!* She pulled out everything in her wardrobe she thought most eye-catching: the micro-mini *sans panties*, three-inch pumps and her totally fav tank top—black, taut, trimmed in pink lace and the message, "Thank God I'm Pretty," across the chest. Jane's ensemble had a message that was indeed hard to miss. But not wanting to be outdone, she wasn't finished. To compensate for reservation in amount of clothing, she doubled up on make-up.

When she found her friend at the club, they commenced the evening's adventure with *two* shots each of tequila. By the time our superstar arrived an hour later, Jane's few inhibitions were long gone and she all but jumped in his lap. Before long, the two were on the dance floor, some would say dancing obscenely, but it was still just two kids having fun.

By the end of the night, Chrissy was nervously combing the nightclub for Jane, thinking she'd been ditched without a ride home. Through the sweaty throng, and with mounting disconcertion, she thought she recognized Dick sitting in a booth with Jane's hair bobbing in and out of view at the edge of the table.

Oh licentious my!

Fortunately, or unfortunately, she did find Jane, in a…uh-hum…a compromising position.

She looked away but stayed near the table so she wouldn't lose sight of Jane again. The moment Jane took a break to go to the restroom, Chrissy grabbed her and said, "I'm outta here! Are you coming or not?"

"Not. Never!" Jane giggled and almost fell over.

"I'm trashed and I can still tell you're making a fool of yourself. You should come home now."

"I'm not going anywhere. This is the chance I've been waiting for!" Jane slurred.

"Chance for what?" Chrissy grumbled as she left Jane in the blur of drunks and smoke.

The next afternoon, Jane rushed to Chrissy's apartment. With her make-up smeared, same clothes—now wrinkled—and crying, she poured into Chrissy's arms and screamed,

"He raped me."

"He what?" Chrissy looked astounded. "You had sex? I mean, did you leave with him? What happened?" she stammered trying to piece together what already appeared to be *Hump*ty *Dump*ty's shell, so to speak.

"We went to a hotel and we fooled around, and then we went to sleep. And then suddenly I woke up and he was inside me!"

"Slow down! I saw what you were doing in the nightclub. *That* was already having sex. But you're saying he raped you when you went to spend the night with him? I don't get it," Chrissy said, feeling increasingly ill.

"God, what's with the 'tude? You're acting like you're on his side. I just told you he raped me!"

"OK, OK. Tell me again. Line by line, what happened."

"We were at the club and drinking and dancing, and...."

"I saw that part clearly," Chrissy interrupted.

"OK, then later at the hotel we messed around and I told him I didn't want to have sex with him, and he said fine. So then we went to sleep and when I woke up he was inside me."

"So what did you do?"

"I left."

"But, you said he was *raping* you! Did you kick, scream, scratch him?"

"Well, no, I didn't want to hurt him."

"You didn't want to hurt someone who was raping you?" Chrissy felt depraved just being a part of the conversation.

"Well, I…I guess I didn't know what to make of it. I think, or I thought, maybe I might want to see him again or see if it could turn into something, but I just didn't want to go all the way yet. But not now. I'm going to call the police and I'm going to sue him!"

I won't have the reader endure any more of this execrable story, which occurs in this or milder forms more often than one would care to believe. Bars and nightclubs all over the world (and of all countries where I've seen this, it's generally the worst in the U.S.—not sure about all the reasons why, but I have a few ideas) are full of stories along these lines every night of the week.

I don't consider myself ascetic when I say that young people, booze and late nights is a combo advised only for those looking for trouble. Just like my salsa teacher used to say: *Ain't nothin' open after midnight 'cept your legs…so get home before the stroke of twelve!*

Lesson

As I mentioned in the introduction, not all Janes are all-together. However, with the depth of her stupidity and degenerate behavior, the Jane in our story hardly qualifies as "Jane." I'd rather confine her to the she-Dick department. However, for the sake of the lesson and how it can benefit others—those more intelligent and less morally depraved—we'll leave her here and discuss her behavior when encountering Dick.

Was she raped? Was she not? Oh, Lord, where's King Solomon when you need him?

Courts, with samples of every fluid running in the human body, can't honestly figure out this one. How could it be proven? In this scenario, it gets down to the word of two vacuous human beings and who's telling the truth. But I can tell you one thing, if the Dick in this situation is a minority and his partner isn't, whether or not he's guilty, he's going to need a team of the best attorneys money can buy, and then he'll still probably do time. (No ruffled feathers, please. Just sayin' it like it is.)

Fortunately, we don't have to judge either of these pitiful characters. What we can do is look at the lessons offered and apply them in our life's journey. This is like walking through a mine field, so before any of us lose a foot, let's diffuse a few of the bombs:

1) If a woman says no to one extremely intimate activity and yes to another, that means "yes" to that and "no" to the other. No one has the right to assume "yes" to that means "yes" to the other.

2) Yes, a woman has a right to spend the night with a man in the same bed without him assuming he can have intercourse with her.
3) Yes, a woman can dress however it pleases her as long as it's legal.

Yet this scenario reminds me of the pedestrian who steps off the curb in the crosswalk in front of a car going 50 mph and protests, "But I had the right-of-way!" as he or she is carted off in an ambulance. Even if you're right, you still lose. So let's look at how we can keep our little toes on the sidewalk and let those fast cars whiz by without smashing us.

We've all heard the proverb:

If it walks like a duck and talks like a duck....

Or more apropos...

If it walks like a skanky slut and talks like a skanky slut....

Or specifically...

If a woman goes out to a bar half-dressed, gets drunk and/or high and has oral sex with a stranger (or well-known friend, for that matter) in public before going to a hotel room with him—she is not asking—she is imploring trouble to ravage her. Picture a little bunny hopping through the still desert night with a sign that says, "Dinner," between her floppy ears and looking for coyotes with whom she can frolic under the moonlight.

Get fucking real, Jane! Literally.

Communication can be difficult even when it's between sober, intelligent people. If you want to stay out of infectious and dangerous scenarios, don't send seriously contradictory signals. You simply can't expect to walk like a duck, talk like a duck and have a man think, "Hmm, this must be the rare and glorious American Eagle."

I won't belabor this point because we probably already have people in a tizzy on both sides, but take this sound advice: Only send signals for what you want. Be clear and be careful.

The vendor selling cherries doesn't advertise nuts!

–ALLIE CHEE

CHAPTER 4

THE DICK YOU KNOW

We've addressed how to deal with the random Dick one encounters moving through life: at the grocery store, in a bar, around the way. That Dick is generally the easiest to identify and the easiest to avoid—or, if already entangled, to get rid of.

Let's address what to do when someone who is already in your circle of acquaintances—someone you had initial reason to trust (or so you thought)—turns out to be a Dick.

Our first character earns the title "Swami Dick" (sounds like something requiring a trip to the local pharmacy to make it go away!)

Swami Dick

He was the leader of the largest prayer group in a small community. Jane was a sweet, loving woman interested in a spiritual connection in a monogamous relationship. She knew he wasn't married because a few of his exes were in the group and had informed her of his status.

Ugh!

You can already see where this is going. Teachers and leaders getting action with their students and followers is like taking candy from a baby. Take heed if your teacher hits on you immediately, or if he has exes in his ranks. This is the sound of a snake rattling, and the mare shows her filly to run if she hears that foreboding sound.

Jane became more and more devout in her practice, praying every day, sometimes for hours, and going on all the retreats around the world with the group.

When he first invited her to his house after prayer group one evening, she was thrilled, though she had some nagging doubts. Was this just another meditation practice, or was he interested in her? He wasn't her type physically. She usually took her men like she took her chocolate: extra dark and strong. He was pasty, had a small frame and let's just say he was "nice looking." But none of that mattered to her. He was a spiritual leader, had dedicated his life to helping people and that was more than enough—she fell in love before their first night together.

She was surprised by his passion. When she arrived on that first evening, he had placed ylang-ylang candles at the front door and all the way up the stairs leading to the bedroom looking over the valley. He had trays of fruits, nuts and sweets at the side of the bed. He wanted to have sex until the sun rose. Anyone that spiritually connected would be a passionate, giving person. He was channeling ineffable energy! She'd found her life partner.

As the weeks progressed, she fell more and more in love. She didn't get to see him as often as she liked, though. He needed time alone for spiritual contemplation, to clear his mind for his work, to recover his energy from his travels.

Sure, time alone is important. We can buy that, for now.

After he'd been travelling for a week, she naturally expected that since he returned on a Friday night, he'd call her and she'd pick him up at the airport or at least meet him later at his place. Friday morning came and went without a call, an email or a text, so she left a message that remained unreturned.

"He's so busy," she thought, "and didn't he say that he doesn't like to send text messages?" she consoled herself. "Of course he'll call when he gets home, so I won't make plans for tonight."

Doesn't the lamb, too, follow the shepherd unquestioningly to the bitter end?

At 8:00 PM, well after he should have arrived, she called him. "Oh, hi. Yes, I'd love to see you. I just need time to myself after my big week," he said.

Let's cut in right here and now. He's lost me. Are any of you buying this tiresome BS? If you are, you should start a *Go, Jane! Support Group* and study this book for your kick-off meeting. Back to our story....

The next day he called and asked her to come over for lunch... *lunch!* That isn't handwriting on the wall, it's a neon sign.

Over their meal he explained that with the spiritual heights he climbed, he just didn't have the energy to give to her what she needed—that she *deserved!*

He said that he lived, almost literally, between two worlds. He had one foot on earth and one in the spiritual realm. Yet he offered a solution.

"You should take other lovers. No, don't look surprised. I love you, but I'm just not enough for you. Take one, two, black, white. It's all about love anyway. I'm not selfish. I wouldn't be living in the spirit if I tried to contain you. You're suuuch a good person. I want you to be happy."

Lesson

I wish I'd been there to slap that Dick's pizzle into the spiritual realm along with that one foot. Give us a break, man! This Jane was admittedly naïve and utterly duped. Let's look at the lessons from our dear sister's experience:

First, when he is your lover and the compliment he gives you is, "You're suuuch a good person," the translation is, "Go away quietly."

Next, is there really a man on earth, who, if truly in love with a woman, needs his space "spiritually" after a weeklong trip? Janes of the world, listen up. The answer is no. Hell no! There are no exceptions. Ah, but he's a high priest, a guru, a martial arts teacher, an esteemed politician you say? That only means that he might have cheated on you with a woman and perhaps a teenage boy during the week and will still want you upon his return.

Go, Jane!

Rumor has it that women have about 60,000 thoughts per day and men have about 12,000. And guess what? About 11,000 of men's 12,000 are about S.E.X. There's nothing wrong with that. Again, it's nature. But *no way* does a man in love gone a week want to spend the night alone, rather than potentially having sex all night. Uh, like, hell no! Not buying it. Not for a second, unless he's older—around 85 at least. And even then, wouldn't he want to cuddle?

If he was gone for a week, that means he has about 77,000 backed-up sex thoughts (which masturbating did not lessen) and even if he doesn't have the energy for romance and passion, he at the very least wants the woman he loves in bed next to him to keep him warm and hold him. Period. (And even if exhausted beyond movement, what do you think the odds are that he would turn down a blow job from his beloved?)

If your man ever returns from a week away and then needs his space, you should call your girlfriends and go out. Go to the spa, get back in the gym and do all the other things you do when you break up—because it's coming.

OK, maybe not right away. There could be a miraculous healing. But take my word for it: Even if his words are with you now, his thoughts are *not*.

And I'm just getting started ripping this Dick a new one. On to the next point. "You should take another lover." Hello, Jane, do we have more than one neuron firing at the same time? Let's get those things working in unison. I hear that omega-3s can help with that.

A man deeply in love, even if attracted to other women, usually doesn't want other lovers for himself or his woman.

OK, hand-brake stop!

Maybe many of them would like to have other lovers, but they act like they don't, nor do they pursue it, because they love their woman and know they'd lose her if they did—or at least out of respect for family or their personal preference or code of ethics.

If we Janes are honest, sure there are times we look at a guy and think, "Damn, I'd like that beefcake to throw me on all fours and drive it home," but we don't do it, for our own list of reasons. Just human nature, Jane; don't freak out. But we've left something hanging. Back to this little Dick at hand.

A Dick in love can easily say he loves his woman and then take other lovers. But *even a Dick* doesn't want his woman to have other lovers (unless those other lovers are female—and that's a different story we're not going to talk about). If that's your gig, stop reading this book and see if you and your love circle can get scheduled on a psychobabble talk show; or better, you might enjoy your summers in the bucolic villages of The Canary Islands.

The rapscallion who tells you he wants you to take another lover is not only saying that he wants to take other lovers, he really is saying you need not exist. Dump that sucker, Jane. Flee before he gives you VD.

> *An open marriage is nature's way of telling you that you need a divorce.*
> **–ANN LANDERS**

P.S. I almost forgot to address the fact that *she called him* the night he got home from the trip. Jane, don't do that. He's been out of town. You already called once. If you have to hunt your man like a wild boar, forget it. We're in the modern world, but him still Tarzan, you still Jane. And if you listen to me, Jane will wind up with Tarzan rather than Dick.

"But he's shy," you say?

No he's not. Ask any man.

I asked a trusted Dick, and he said, "Oh, yea, after he's bagged a chick, even the most timid Dick is over it. As a matter of fact, many dudes who started out shy become Super Dick after they've finally had sex with a chick."

It's alarming to hear that kind of blunt, crude talk—especially if you've been entangled with this type of Dick and were excusing his behavior. But if we keep our heads up our asses, it only leads to continued trouble with Dicks, when what we need to do is keep our heads clear. We need to stop making excuses for Dicks in an attempt to get something that we will never get, and stay healthy and available for all the good men out there to come into our lives.

Don't make up lame excuses for why they haven't called. Always remember: After you've done the shagnasty, their intimidation shrivels like a penis in a swimming pool.

For many, this concept takes a while to sink in, so it merits repetition. He's not shy—and even if he is, he still has a penis. He's not intimidated by your beauty or money or intelligence—and even if he is, he still thinks frequently about the needs of his penis. He's not really tied up at work, and even if he is, he'd still want you to meet him at his office, hide under his desk and play with his penis.

"*Oh, but he's so busy when he travels for work,*" you say.

Upon concluding his campaign in Egypt and preparing to return to France, Napoleon sent a letter to his wife, Josephine, which said:

J'arrive. Ne te lave pas. (I'm coming. Don't wash.)

Forget the fetish. The point is that while 2,000 miles away (on horseback) and wrapping up a busy invasion, Napoleon found time to write to his wife.

Perhaps your man has more on his plate than Napoleon? Even with his phone attached to his hand, he doesn't have time to send a text? Hmm.

If he returns from travel, weekend or not, and he hasn't called, go out with your friends, or stay home and do doodle art, or diddle yourself. Anything, but for god's sake, don't look pathetic and throw yourself at him. You're headed for the end when you do that, so why not jump off early and spare yourself the wasted energy and hurt.

Don't misunderstand. Women can call men. Women can initiate. Women can ask men on dates, can be on top. Women can even propose to men! BUT not if the man is giving you the cold shoulder. Get a grip. And remember to add flaxseed oil to your shake in the morning.

So how did the Swami Dick story end? Jane finally got the hint and cut off the relationship. Then, after he'd been traveling for several days—alone—he came home and called our Jane, inviting her to dinner, to "pray," and to talk about their split. Her best friend knew where this was going, and since Jane had already used her own strength once to leave, her friend decided to prop her up in the storm, and confronted her.

"What do you think will happen at dinner? What will be said that hasn't already been said?"

"I just need closure."

"You have closure. You know who he is and what he wants—and doesn't want."

"But I need to hear it from him. I haven't heard his side."

"Why do you need to hear his side? You know your side, and that's enough."

"I have to do this."

"What you mean is you hope that you'll go, you'll have great sex, and he will tell you it was a huge mistake and that he loves you and can't live without you by his side. Right?"

"I don't know. I can't say," and she started to cry.

"That means, yes, you hope all that happens. But it won't. Except for the part about having sex."

"How do you know that? How do you know what he'll say?"

"I don't. But you do. You've already heard the things he has to say, and it led you to break it off. And what was his reaction? Did he run to your doorstep with flowers, say that you were mistaken, that he loves you, cares for you and wants you in his life?"

"No, but he called after he thought about it for a week and now he wants to have dinner."

"And you go running."

Blech!

Her friend then encouraged Jane to call Dick, explain that she'd be happy to meet him for lunch *in a restaurant* any time in the next few days to discuss their relationship further.

And so it came to pass, the miracle happened and Jane made the call! She was heartbroken and so desperately wanted to see him, even if it was only to be used. Yet somehow she broke an old pattern and found the strength to resist. We've all been in this position to some degree and know how difficult it can be to acknowledge the truth of the situation and restrain ourselves.

What happened when she called him? He explained that, yes, well, he'd be traveling for a couple of lectures over the next few weeks and his schedule was kinda tight, and so he'd call again when he was settled in at home again.

Does that sound like a man pining away for his lost love? She had her closure—without being used again in the process. She got outta there—better later than never.

He who is outside the door already has the hard part of his [her] journey behind him [her].
–DUTCH PROVERB

Pulpit Dick
(It sounds gross, too... and it is)

Some Dicks we encounter are on the fringe of our circle of acquaintances, but some are deeper in the circle: someone with whom you work, for example, or who holds a position of power.

A preacher in Texas led a large, devoted congregation. One of the most devoted of the devotees was his secretary. She swooned when he walked in the room. She heard a chorus of angels when he stepped to the pulpit. She was *in love*. The only problem—he was married.

"My wife doesn't understand me. I don't know how I was ever fooled by her. She was just after my money and wanted to share in my limelight," Dick explained. On and on he went, ever more persuasive that his wife had essentially conned him and that the decision to divorce was inspired—probably the most holy decision he'd ever made. *God hates divorce but he hates livin' a lie just as much!* was his mantra.

Any priest or shaman must be presumed guilty until proved innocent.
–ROBERT HEINLEIN

So Jane fell into a full-blown affair with the married preacher, banking on the imminent divorce. Lo! and behold, the divorce came, and he did marry that secretary. But wait! You haven't heard the good part yet.

She was his fourth wife!

Jesus, Mary and Joseph!

Does that end our happy saga (or end his devoted congregation)? *Hello! Anyone home? I guess they're focusing on the message, not the messenger.* Not even close. Because after a couple of years, and with an even greater following, that preacher was getting a bit bored with the secretary when a really devoted member of the choir caught his eye. Know where this is going? Correct. Wife number four was dumped and we don't know what happened with sucker number five. Any ideas?

> *A man who marries his mistress leaves a vacancy in that position.*
> **–OSCAR WILDE**

[And nature loathes a vacancy.]

Lesson

Jane, under what rock have you been hiding? Come out for some fresh air and healing sunlight! If he cheats on another woman to be with you, consider:

a) Do you really want to be with someone whose word is horseshit?
b) Do you really think he won't cheat on you? (If somehow he doesn't cheat on you, that's great. Call the *Guinness Book of Records* and we'll see your happy wedding picture next to the photo of the guy who ate 1,000 hot dogs in one minute.)

I can already hear some Janes.

"But he explained the problem with their relationship: *She's* been cheating on *him*!"

Do you believe that? 50/50 chance. And so what if she's cheating on him? If he fools around before he gets his divorce, it makes him a cheater, too.

"But he's been separated for three months!"

Separated—not divorced. Do you know how many separated people get back together after they've gotten out their frustration by copulating with a few unsuspecting suckers? This Jane has had Dicks tell her that they were separated while they were simply sleeping in a separate bedroom from their wife in their home. *Dick, please! Inflict yourself on someone else and call me when the divorce is long over!*

Maybe you're thinking, "But he says his girlfriend/wife is awful (a drunk, let herself go, a raging bitch, a psycho) and I'm great. He'd *never* do that to me!"

Again, we have a few things to consider: a) he chose her, b) do you want a man who speaks of his spouse to others with those words (even if they are true)?, and c) yes, he will do that to you. You are special. But he's a Dick if he's hitting on you while in a commitment with someone else.

Let us repeat and refer back to the cosmic law that how things begin is often indicative of things to come. It doesn't matter how beautiful, loving and intelligent you are; I don't care how big your boobs are, how round your booty is, what a great mother you'd make or how well you cook—he's a Dick and will cheat on you. If he doesn't, it's a miracle. Miracles do happen—but do you really want to waste your precious time banking on a long shot, or would you rather spend a bit more time alone while you wait for someone with your lifestyle, energy level and values?

Since many of us have ignored or will ignore this advice in the future, at least consider this: There are many people who have been in living hell, tortured for years in their rotten marriages with a horrible choice in a partner that they made when far too young or stupid to know better, and they probably haven't had (good, if any) sex in a long time. We give them that, and feel for them.

If you believe there is deep potential and your ensnared candidate is truly a special character, then tell him you'd love to be friends with him while he goes through his divorce and you look forward, if the relationship continues to grow positively, to a wonderful sex life together *after* he's divorced. If he doesn't agree with a smile, go back to the beginning of this chapter, reread and ignore this last paragraph.

He that walketh with wise men shall be wise;
but a companion of fools shall be destroyed.
–PROVERBS 13:20

She who sleeps with the loyal man shall beget sweet honey;
but a companion of the wandering canine
shall contract fleas.
–ALLIE CHEE 5'8"

Often Dicks prey on Jane with the hope of exploiting her sexually; other times it's just for money or simply the desire to exert control or to try to comfort themselves with a false sense of power in their miserable, limp existence.

In this next story, Dick was looking for a free ride.

Swingin' Dick

Jane had become close friends with her golf coach. Over the months and years he told her the intricacies of his life and she confided all her secret joys and hopes. They were almost like brother and sister. He knew she'd been increasingly dissatisfied with her 20-year corporate career and had saved fastidiously for the time when she could start her own business. One day, he approached her with a brainstorm to open a golf shop. *It will make mountains of money—it may take a year or two—but this will be just the start. We will franchise the idea later. We'll both be millionaires doing something we love.*

Uh, there's just one thing. He didn't have much cash (what with the divorce and all those child support payments—he really got screwed by that sneaky ex), so Jane needed to pony up the dough. Oh, yeah, another thing…since he was working so hard to pay his bills—this was just at the beginning, mind you—she was going to need to do most of the start-up work. The contract…what contract? They'd been friends for years, and even if they weren't like family, didn't they both believe strongly in karma?

Jane agreed—and in less than a year she'd lost the business, her time, her savings and (fortunately), her golf "friend."

Lesson

This is a good time to look back to nature. Insects and flowers have a beautiful symbiotic relationship. Plants and flowers offer support and the nutrition needed by the insects, and the insects help plants procreate by dispersing their pollen. So far, a lovely story resembling a lifelong friendship.

However, just as in the human realm, in the plant kingdom there are shysters. Take the Venus Flytrap, for example. This plant is found in nitrogen-poor environments, usually swampy, boggy places. The leaves are shaped like hearts and appear to offer the support and nutrients insects expect from a plant. When an unsuspecting insect lands on the Venus Flytrap, the leaves snap shut, turn into a stomach and digest the poor critter.

Do you see any parallels between the story of the Venus Flytrap and Jane with her Swingin' Dick friend? The insect wouldn't have been so easily duped if its predator had been a sparrow; it knows that birds eat insects. However, since the organism was cleverly disguised as something that supports insects, it was trapped and consumed.

If you're going to invest all your money and a lot of your time, start a business by yourself or with someone who has something to contribute, aside from a supposed lifelong friendship as collateral. Further, always—and I mean always—get everything in writing and before you sign, have an unbiased, *qualified* third-party review the documents.

In love, business and all of life: If you commit to something with a person who has nothing to lose and you have something to lose— guess what? You'll lose. Before you let that happen, lose that Dick!

The palest ink is better than the sharpest memory.
–ANCIENT CHINESE PROVERB

Slick Willy

Jane had just broken up with her boyfriend and was bummed out. "Well, there's always salsa," she said and dragged herself to class at the Cha Cha Chica restaurant.

She joined the group with a heavy heart and slow feet. She was clumsy and limp in her form and her practice partners were becoming irritated. She decided to skip the second half of class and go home to mourn when she looked up and made eye contact with *him*. He was sitting at the bar watching the class. Short, skinny, balding, glasses—not the usual slick *salsero*. Yet something in his eyes said to her, "Yes, I can dance—*very* well. And, yes, you and I will dance—and we will do more than that."

Jane turned back to her partner in the class with a refreshed spirit and new step in her stride. In a single measure of music she was back to her old self. Whew, she was up, down and around the floor until the class ended. Sweaty, and with a smile on her face, she walked to a bench and sat down to change out of her dance shoes. When she looked up there *he* was.

"Put them back on," he smiled.

She put them back on.

"Are you a good dancer?" she asked, but knew the answer.

He held out his hand to take hers.

"You're a teacher?" Jane asked, but knew the answer.

He led her to the dance floor.

Let's take a break from our little fiesta right here and talk about this.

So far, so good. This story is already full of fun and passion. There's only one red flag. Any clues? Yes, Jane, you're learning. She is fresh out of a relationship and hurting. Dancing, good idea. Dancing with someone really good, great idea. But will she leave it at that? Let's find out.

He took her to places on the floor she'd never been. After an hour she'd forgotten her ex completely and was head-over-heels, so to speak. He asked her if she had a boyfriend or husband. "No," she smiled, vaguely remembering a face that had mattered that morning.

She asked him if he had a girlfriend. "I'm in the middle of a divorce," he answered, "and I already have my own place."

Ay, caramba! Here we go.

They spent that first night together and she was as swept away in bed as she was on the floor. They spent a few months living almost like husband and wife. She had a *drawer* there. She cooked meals in his kitchen. They went dancing almost every night.

One morning when he left for work, the drawer in the night stand below "her drawer" was open, just a crack, and she saw a greeting card with hearts on it. It wasn't snooping, she figured. It was, after all, almost her nightstand and she was sort of living there, no? Maybe he intended it as a surprise for her?

The card, dated just a few days earlier, had a printed message on the front: "I love you." The inside, handwritten message spoke of a passionate encounter and a loving reunion.

Tears streaming down her face, furious and heartbroken, she called her best friend.

"He's cheating on me!" she screamed.

"With who?" her friend inquired.

"With his wife!"

Did you hear the mambo record scratch?

Lesson

We've covered it already, so we know the first thing Jane should do: Pull her head out of her *culo* so she can breathe.

It's just like sitting in a plane. We've heard the instructions in case problems occur, but it's important to review them every time.

Here are a few phrases that should ring in your ears like the roar of a lion ringing in the gazelle's:

- I'm thinking about a divorce.
- I'm separated.
- I'm filing next week.
- I'm meeting with my lawyer.
- We're working on a settlement.
- It was final last month.

That dancin' fool can't help but be a Dick now. You know why, since we've gone over it, so stay away! Let him heal rather than allow him to drag you into his suffering and love triangles.

What is true by firelight is not always true by daylight.
—**FRENCH PROVERB**

CDO (Chief Dick Officer)

You have a fabulous new job in a Fortune 500 company, and despite your experience and credentials, you were really nervous when you started. However, the CEO himself took you under his wing and was so kind and helpful that soon you were learning the ropes and anticipating years of promotions and growing stock options. The CEO is so nice, in fact, that he covers for you when you make mistakes and even offers to help you in his office—after hours—just so you can quickly assimilate all the business lingo and learn the ropes. He puts his arm around you, holds you closely and says that if you are a quick study, that first big raise might be just around the corner.

Lesson

Anyone thinking about that Venus Flytrap we discussed earlier?

Go, Jane!

First big raise, huh? Maybe, but something else is going up in the air! A Dick, Jane! Nobody gets something for nothing. Not in the office, not in the neighborhood, not in life. If you want to really get tangled up in a tar baby, get involved in this kind of situation at work.

If you want to avoid this situation, proceed with caution when receiving offers for "special help," benefits you know are not a part of your job position, and especially any social invitations along the lines of "a quick drink" after work!

> *"(S)he who depends on (her)himself will attain the greatest happiness."*
> **–ANCIENT CHINESE PROVERB**

Lame Dick

Jane hadn't seen Dick and Angelina in months. Angelina had been a high school buddy and her roommate through college. Angelina and Dick met before graduation and were married a year later. Even after Dick and Ang got married, the three of them were inseparable. When Ang had their first kid, they slowly stopped doing the things that had held them together. First they stopped their bike tours around the lake on Saturday mornings. Then they stopped hiking and grilling by the pool afterwards on Sundays. As happens all the time with friends, they grew apart.

Ang and Dick's second child had just turned six months old when Ang called to invite Jane for dinner. Jane was thrilled, but noticed that her friend sounded...*something*. Tired? Aggressive? Anyway, not her old self. "Obviously!" Jane thought. "Two kids, one a baby. She's low on energy."

They decided on their old usual: grill chicken, drink beer. Jane arrived early with a six-pack of Moretti, another old favorite.

They sat on the deck drinking and watching the sunset. Jane was happy to see them, but there was a tension that even the oncoming buzz wasn't lightening. The baby started to cry and Ang left to feed her, telling Jane and Dick to start the grill.

Dick fired up the coals while Jane cut the chicken. When she brought it outside, Dick handed her the tongs.

As she arranged the pieces on the hot grill, Dick came up behind her and offered a bright smile and held up a beer.

Reader Jane, you can guess what happened next.

She recoiled. "What the hell, Dick?"

"What?' he asked, with a "Who, me?" look on his face.

"What the hell was that? Ang is my best friend."

"It was nothing, Jane, forget it. I'm going to run and help tuck in the kids."

Jane fought back her disgust and made light talk through dinner. When they'd finished, she said something about needing to get up early—and practically ran from the house.

She never spoke with either one of them again.

Lesson

Jane, what would you do? This is tough. Guess what I would do. Napalm? No, not this time. But my answer wouldn't be to do nothing.

I'd leave the dinner immediately. I'd tell the hostess that I needed to leave—an important matter. Later I'd meet my friend and, with just the two of us, I'd tell her this:

Girl, you're married to a big ole Dick. That dog is marking every bush in town. Get a clue, get a life and get rid of him.

Just kidding. That's what I'd want to say.

What I'd really say is:

"I'm in a rotten position that's already cost me one friendship. Dick said inappropriate things to me and touched me in an inappropriate way. I know you have a marriage and two kids to consider. I don't know what I would do in your position, and what you do is not my business. The only thing that is my business is that he got me tangled up in what is clearly his problem.

"You know me; I've never swept things under the rug. My only choice was to tell you. I'll never see you at your house—or with him—again. Since he was willing to do that, he'll probably be willing to lie to you about what happened. You'll know the truth in your heart—maybe now, maybe later. If you choose to stay friends with me, which I hope, I'm here."

What would happen then? The wife would likely run back to Dick in tears, and he would tell her: "Jane confided in me how she was jealous of us, the family life we have that has for some reason been elusive for her, and then, well, I gave her an innocent hug to console her and she tried to kiss me."

Angelina would probably discover the truth at some point when she found lipstick on her husband's shirt or a love note e-card in his inbox. Then again, maybe it was a one-time loss of consciousness? Right! And 19-year-old milkmaids shack up with Hugh Hefner because of their deep spiritual connection (for further information, refer to *Swami Dick* and *Big Shot Dick*).

Broke Dick

Jane had figured out that home was not a safe place to be at a very young age. Her mother was alcoholic and her father was long gone before she was born. The string of men who paraded through her mother's room each had their particularly nasty characteristic. She was now 15, and it was time to go. Fortunately, her Aunt Tanya—only 10 years older—had a small apartment and opened her doors and loving arms to Jane.

Life for the two women was fun and productive. They both had jobs, so the rent was always paid. They both loved to cook and clean, so they ate well, and the place? Well, it was safe, and that was good enough. Life for Jane was more stable and safe than it had ever been.

After dinner one evening, Tanya said she needed to have a talk with Jane. And everyone knows, whether it's your boss, your parent or your neighbor, when they say, "We need to have a talk," you're probably not going to like what they say.

"You know Dick, the guy from the gym I've been seeing a little bit? Well, it's gotten a little more serious. He wants to move in."

Jane knew it had been too good to be true. Her Auntie was kind to her, but life had taught her that everyone was out for number one and a good thing never lasted.

"I'm not asking you to move out! I'm asking if it's OK with you if he shares the place with us. It will be a little tight, but he'll help with the rent, too. "You'll sleep on the sofa, but I'll cut down your rent. Also, when he and I aren't home, you can have the bedroom."

That all sounded fair enough to Jane. Paying less rent would mean she could save faster for her own place.

Dick moved in and life didn't change as much as Jane thought it would. They all went to the gym, they cooked and ate their meals together. Life was still headed in the right direction.

However, the months of sleeping on the sofa began to take a toll and had Jane's back in knots. She would go home straight from the gym to get at least three or four hours of sleep in the real bed when Dick and Tanya were working. Shortly after the new arrangement started, Jane decided that she needed her own space.

When she told them a few days later that she was planning to move soon, Jane was surprised that not only Tanya protested, but so did Dick. He'd been really sweet in the last few weeks.

"Alright, alright. I can't leave right away, even if I wanted to. I don't have the money, so you're stuck with me for a little while longer."

Coming home from the gym a few weeks later, Dick slammed down his bag and let out a fuming sigh. "Boss fired me today. We got into it, and he told me to walk."

Both women assured him that he'd find other work, that they'd cover his rent while he was unemployed and that everything would be all right. But Jane knew it wouldn't be. She'd seen this routine too many times.

Dick didn't get up early the next day to go look for a job as Tanya would—but Jane expected this: He ran out the door in his gym clothes and returned two hours later, sweaty, with a 12-pack in hand.

"Beer?" Jane asked. "What's up?"

"What do you mean what's up? I'm gonna kick back a few days before I beat the streets again."

Jane tried to warn her aunt. "Tanya, he's your boyfriend, so if I need to scoot I will. But trust me. I've seen it before. Two days of no work will turn into weeks of binge drinking. No one unemployed has good intentions if they spend their first day getting trashed."

"Give him a few days. He'll snap out of it. If he doesn't, we'll deal with it then."

Sure enough, Dick remained unemployed for months, but Jane, well versed with this type of character, never let him off the hook. "You still need to clean up after dinner." "You still need to clean the bathroom on Sunday." "When are you going to *clean yourself up* and go interview?"

"You got quite a mouth on you. Clean, clean, clean. Is that all you can say?" he snapped back.

One early evening, very tired from work and having skipped the gym, Jane went home to crash. She was in the bedroom getting those precious hours of sleep on the bed when the door opened. Assuming Dick had forgotten it was her "room time" and that she was in there sleeping, she said, "Hey, Dick. Give me an hour and I'll be out of here."

He didn't say anything and she felt the bed move slightly. She was groggy but figured out in the second she had to think that it must be her aunt.

"It's me," he said.

Suddenly wide awake, she bolted up. Before she could run, he had her pinned.

Horrified and shocked, she froze. Who was this? Dick? Can't be. My God. Help!

She finally screamed. How long had it been? Five seconds? A minute? Ten minutes? She screamed and screamed. He put his hands over her mouth, but she bit his fingers and screamed some more. And not in vain.

The bedroom door slammed open and a dark figure raced through the room toward them swinging a baseball bat.

Repulsed and relieved in equal amounts, Tanya moved Dick's unconscious body away from Jane and they fled the apartment.

When they returned, Dick was gone.

Lesson

We could devote an entire book to the lessons to be learned from this story, but we're going to focus on one: the lesson of how to stop this criminal—immediately. When Jane told me her story over a coffee at Starbucks, of course her aunt knew, but it was the first time she'd talked about it with anyone else. *Anyone.*

Of course you can see the obvious implication: She didn't tell the police.

I know there are a lot of Janes reading this and reliving the way they were violated. Know at least this: You're hardly alone and it's not your fault. Actually, those who remain untouched in any way by this kind of demonic man are fewer than you'd think. And let's look at one of the big reasons why. We've already addressed it. Most men are at least decent if not genuine, wonderful people. But the twisted and sick ones are allowed to run loose, leaving a wake of destruction behind them.

Jane was incredibly blessed. Fortune had her aunt arrive home early that night. A family member witnessed the crime and came immediately to the defense.

Many girls never get help or go for help—at the time of the crime, or ever. Most boys never go for help. But then, how many children go to their mothers or guardians asking for help when their fathers, grandfathers, stepfathers and mother's boyfriends mishandle or rape them, only to hear:

- You're just jealous.
- Stop making up lies.
- What did you do to provoke it?
- You caused it.

More than we want to believe. I personally know dozens of men and women who've told me their stories of abuse, and probably hundreds more who have a story but haven't talked about it.

In high school, my best friend told her mother that her father was raping her. Her mother said, "I don't know what you're talking about. We've got enough to worry about without you making trouble."

Another friend told her mother that her father, her stepfather *and* her grandfather had all abused her in some way. Her mother's answer: "Oh, it happened to me, too," and then carried on with "family life" as usual.

The Dick You Know

I could go on, but here's the most important fact: *Not one* of these people who confided their story to me ever reported the crimes. The list of reasons they didn't is long, and involves deep spiritual and psychological work. But shame, fear and guilt are the primary reasons.

Further, many of them were forced as children to continue to live with, spend holidays with and travel with the very people who'd committed heinous crimes against them. In a most terrible kind of torture, they had to act friendly—like they were happy to see their attackers at Easter dinner or their eighth-grade graduation ceremony. Sister, I've been there…and it's no place to be.[5]

So what is wrong with these people?

Who am I referring to? Forget the criminal—that's a twisted human who needs to be in a padded room, or behind bars or maybe

---

[5] True to my nuclear style, I told everyone in my family of being abused by my mother's father when I was 8 and refused to go anywhere he would be (meaning many family functions)—though everyone else continued to participate in family functions with him. At 19, I called the Dallas Police Department to report the crimes against me 15 years earlier and four other women in the family (three of them adults who'd never spoken out to protect their children), but I was told, bluntly, "It's past the statute of limitations—can't help ya." And that was that. *That* was Texas in the '80s. Hopefully things are changing—but if they aren't, all the more reason for women to learn to protect themselves from Dicks—the point of this book.

castrated Sharia-style. Not the victims; often they're too young or too traumatized to talk. I'm referring to the weak slobs who know about someone in their circle hurting someone—especially a child—who fail to stop or report it. They are the criminals known as *accomplices*.

Remember how easy it is to help, to bring change, to save lives? Three little buttons:

9-1-1.

If there were a rabid dog running in their house, biting people, what would they do?

9-1-1.

That's just a dog and just a bite. So what should they do when someone they know hurts someone they know?

911.

If for whatever reason 911 doesn't do the trick (it doesn't always, for varying reasons), you have to take action yourself. Not vigilante! Just space—*lots of space*. Do whatever necessary to flee the situation.

Dr. Dick

Jane, brought up in a conservative, religious Southern town, was a shy, reserved girl of 17. Despite being a cheerleader, very popular and beautiful to boot, she never drank, smoked nor had sex—the three most predictable activities of the in-crowd in Smallville High.

The start of Jane's menstrual cycle hadn't been a horrible scare as it was for many girls in this town of reticent mothers because her best friend had started before her and informed Jane about not only that, but just about everything having to do with the birds and the bees.

What did frighten Jane was the pain she started to experience in her genital area after a week at summer camp. It started as an irritating itch, but after several days she was extremely uncomfortable, scratching herself constantly. Aside from being embarrassing and awkward, the constant scratching made the irritation worse and more sensitive.

She finally told her mother that something was wrong, and her mother was quick to take her to the doctor. Upon doing a visual inspection, he concluded she had herpes.

"Herpes? But don't you get herpes from having sex?" her mother gasped.

"That's right," the doctor answered.

"I've never had sex," Jane cut in, relieved that it wasn't herpes, but still wondering what the problem really could be.

"Well, there's no need to deny it," the doctor answered with a condescending tone and indignant look.

"I know there's no need to deny it," she said looking at her mother for support but finding a blank face. "As I'm telling you, I've never had sex."

"Look, I'm not going to sit here and listen to lies from you, little lady. Virgins don't have herpes. Your lab report will confirm everything, and until then…." Then he motioned toward the door to speed their departure.

"Then I don't have herpes!" she said as he closed the door to his office.

In the hall, her mother said, "Well, where should we go for lunch?"

Jane, accustomed to this familiar response when her father turned verbally abusive, suggested a restaurant along the road home. And she remained silent.

Two days later, Jane's mother received a phone call from the doctor's assistant saying that they needed to see Jane for further tests.

"Yes," her doctor said, grabbing his clipboard and slipping on his reading glasses, "it appears that you have a yeast infection. My assistant will write up the prescription for you," he said with a brisk wave of his hand to dismiss them.

Jane's mother never discussed what happened with Jane, and had no further conversation with the doctor about his behavior. Jane, 20 years after it happened, told me about that event and was still frustrated about what transpired.

Lesson

Jane, it goes without saying the doctor is an arrogant, ignorant Dick. In this story, the mother was the real loser for allowing a Dick to treat her daughter in that manner.

I would suggest several ideas to ponder.

Go, Jane!

Jane was a young woman, proud of her moral code and, further, living in a town where virginity was of utmost importance (though rare) for a young girl. Challenging her virginity in front of her mother was like putting a scarlet letter on her chest. Dr. Dick further undermined Jane's integrity by calling her a liar—again, in front of her mother.

A mother's job is to protect her child, and this was a form of attack. In the physical manifestation, its effects were negligible (other than Jane's additional stress waiting for the correct diagnosis). However, what was the message? It was: It's OK for a Dick in an authority position to tell you who you are—and no matter how wrong they are, you quietly accept it.

Mom...*where's your head at?* It's not OK. It's how people can lose all self-confidence. One instance of it would not necessarily demoralize a person, but repeated it is how talented, wonderful people grow up believing themselves unworthy of love and respect and then go on to create lifetime patterns of abuse for themselves—and for their children.

Jane's mother should have said something along the lines of, "I'm sure you have your reasons to believe what you said. But if my daughter says she hasn't had sex, then she hasn't." Or, "You may or may not be correct in your diagnosis, but you have absolutely no right to speak in an insulting or degrading way to my daughter. We'll be leaving now." Or, my choice—stand up and leave.

Here's something bigger that this story gives us to ponder. Jane, open your mind for a minute and simply read. Just read and consider...

Young girls are naturally modest, as they should be. In our society, we don't run around nude in front of the opposite sex after the age of 2, 3 or maybe 4 years old. Why, then, do women take their newborn, toddler, pre-teen and teenage girls to be looked at and probed by a male doctor? This would be considered a vile offense in many countries of the world. Men who would choose to practice on young girls would not be suspect, they would be considered perverts—perverts to be put behind bars.

Hold on! I'm not saying all doctors are perverts if they probe the vaginas of young girls for a living. I am saying, given the modest, sensitive nature of young girls, why *wouldn't* a mother consider a female doctor for those kinds of issues—and allow the young girl to choose the sex of her doctor when she's older?

Shouldn't that just be common sense? As the old saying goes—what's more rare than common sense?

A final note to consider: I knew a young and extremely handsome, rich man who'd just finished med school (gynecology) and had a large gathering of fellow grads and doctors to his house for a party to celebrate. I heard one of these "intelligent" young doctors in attendance say to the group, "This lucky guy goes to work where we all go to play!" And the entire group burst out laughing and punching each other.

Of course they're not all like that. But think about it.

Twisted Dick

Her interview was scheduled to start at 11:00 AM so Jane arrived at the office at 10:30.

"Trying hard to impress, huh?" Dick laughed as he walked by his secretary's desk and saw Jane, the new candidate, giving her an up-and-down look.

Jane looked at the secretary quizzically, and the secretary winked and motioned with a wave of her hand to blow it off.

At 10:50 AM Dick opened his office door and said, "Well, you didn't get dressed up for nothing. Come on in and let's get started."

Jane couldn't find the word to describe the bizarre behavior and words Dick used throughout the interview. But she didn't care—this was a great company and if she got this position, she'd secure her place in the industry.

"I know how old you are," he said.

"Is that relevant? she asked.

"Ha!" he shouted. "Tell me about your time at your previous company."

Was he doing this on purpose? Was it a part of the interview to see how she'd respond to a person with strange communication skills? She followed along as best she could—and must have passed whatever test he was giving, because she was hired.

After a few months at the company, Jane befriended several people, becoming fairly close with Debbie.

After being out of the office for a week recovering from surgery, Debbie confided in Jane that she'd been out because she'd had reconstructive surgery on her breasts. Dick happened to walk by the break room at that moment and contributed, "Yea, nice boob job."

"She wasn't speaking to you," Jane snapped, shocked at his comment.

"Thanks, Dick," Debbie jumped in.

After he continued on by, Debbie whispered to Jane, "What's wrong with you?"

"With me? What's wrong with you and everyone here? That guy is always popping off with weird, inappropriate comments—and everyone tiptoes around and kisses his ass."

"Oh, that's just Dick. He doesn't mean anything by it."

Months went by and Jane heard that more and more. During a meeting, two women were debating the effectiveness of a new policy introduced in client presentations when a scowling Dick interjected, "We could get going with the meeting if the hens would stop cackling."

Later, when Jane asked one of them how she felt being spoken to in that manner, she answered, "Oh, that's just Dick. Don't take it too seriously."

(Note to Jane: Take it seriously.)

Dick was great at inflicting his colorful comments and disturbed character on all the women in the office without ever doing anything that could really merit a hard correction. He took credit for their projects. He made strange references regarding their appearance. He insulted their work. But he never used outright profanity. He never physically grabbed anyone. But in little ways, he constantly belittled, insulted and degraded the female employees. As is often the case with Dicks, he was sheltered by his position. Since he was the bridge between the regional office and the national office, no one was willing to be the one to take it to upper management.

After eight months at the company, Jane walked in and was greeted by, "Uh, huh, three-inch pumps. We know what that means," and he smiled lecherously.

[A disturbing but valuable note from a notorious Dick who read the manuscript: *This Dick is probing the staff and gauging their responses, looking for the right reaction. The one who smiles back or returns an equally inappropriate comment just might be willing to fuck and merits further probing.* Take heed, Jane.]

"What does that mean?" she asked.

"Better yet, let's talk about the new accounting process for your client," he answered.

"No, let's stick to your topic, my shoes. What does, 'We know what that means,' mean?"

He answered, "Are you in a strange mood this morning, Jane? Maybe you need to take some PTO?"

No, but Dick needs some SKB (swift kick in bollocks).

Lesson

Jane, what do you do in her shoes?

If you blow the whistle, you'll more than likely pay the price. A huge corporation is not going to remove top management because you say he mentioned something about your high heels. Period. You say that he is a hostile, rude and manipulative person creating an uncomfortable environment for all the female employees? Then how come no one else is complaining?

While I would never refrain from exposing a Dick for fear of backlash, your primary goal is to take care of your peace of mind and body. When you consider all the ramifications of attempting to rectify the problem, the size of the offense (extremely difficult to define by law), the people affected (all adults choosing to be there) and the magnitude of the price to be paid by the whistle blower, my first thought would be, screw it. Leave before you become miserable or an accomplice like the rest of the office. Get down the road. There are laws against harassment, but since there aren't you-can't-be-a-Dick laws, the best path would be to move to a high functioning environment.

If you really love the work and know it's an environment in which you could find happiness sans abuse from a Dick, go to HR and get it on record. Their job is to protect everyone, including Dick—*and* you. Probably not, but they may already have a file of complaints on Dick, and yours could finally push them to respond.

If they do not protect you, write his supervisor and HR when you leave, documenting the reasons why. It'll go in the file. One thing I highly suggest (that would not rob your energy) would be to be honest in your exit interview with HR. That goes on record, too.

He that speaks the truth must have one foot in the stirrup.

–TURKISH PROVERB

Pigskin Dick

She went to a public high school in Texas. A typical school in the South, there was the Old Main building and the trailers (temporary buildings) lined up in the grass next to Old Main. There was bussing and racial tension, but—most important of all—there was football. Football players ranked just below angels and on par with the saints in the hearts of the locals. The coach? He was the town god.

Jane was cute, bubbly, the cheerleader type. She would have been a cheerleader, which everyone knew was the best thing a girl at this school could be, except she had no parents taking care of her and no way to get home from practice after school. She would have done better at school, but for the same reasons, she was falling behind in her grades.

Science class was particularly challenging for her. The high school football coach, Dick, taught the class, and asked her to stay late one day to discuss why she was failing. Since she had no one who could help her at home, maybe he could cut a few hours outta the week to tutor her.

With the first few sessions she showed a lot of improvement. On her next test, she scored a B. But when reviewing it, she noticed that a few of her answers were indeed incorrect, yet the coach had not marked them off. After class she approached his desk to discuss. He was busy with other students and just winked at her, "Don't worry, we'll talk about it next time."

During the next tutoring session, he sat close to her, shoulder to shoulder, so they could look over the test together. He slid his hand off the desk and put it on her thigh. She tensed and moved her chair a few inches to put more space between them.

"You're a beautiful girl, you know that?" he said.

"I think I'd better go home," she said, gathering her books and tablet.

He moved toward her, grabbed her harshly, slamming one hand between her legs as he used his other hand to force her face against his.

She pushed him away and he came toward her again. She left her books and backpack, and ran from the room.

For a few days, she stayed home from school "sick." After the shock wore off and the indignation and fury mounted, she decided, "I'm going tell the principal and he'll be fired. Then I can go back to school. I didn't do anything."

If she'd only known.

Amazingly, she gained the courage to return to the great halls of education, march in the principal's office and tell her story. Strength and clarity of that magnitude in a young girl is uncommon.

She waited for the alarms to sound, the cavalry to be summoned, the outcry of disgust and the wave of support from the faculty and other students.

The principal remained silent till she was done, offering nothing in the way of a comforting word or gesture. "Well, that certainly is an interesting story. I think we'd better call Coach in to discuss this with him and get his take on it."

"Bring him in here? I don't want to be in a room with him again. Ever!"

"You've made a heavy accusation there, missy, and Coach has a right to tell his side of the story."

She was forced into an interrogation by the principal and the coach, in which it was determined that he'd been helping her study and she'd misunderstood his actions. If this "scuffle" really happened, where were the scratch marks on him—the bruises and other signs of a fight, of her resistance? She'd best go about her business and try to keep her grades up on her own, because the coach wasn't going to spend his time helping her anymore.

Stunned with the feeling of being abused and betrayed, she walked from class to class like a zombie. She avoided the gym, ran from the cafeteria after lunch and hid in the library during her breaks.

"Unreal! I'm the one they put on trial and punished," she thought to herself.

Then when she was beginning to think it would eventually fade to black as a horrible memory, the captain of the football team spray-painted "SLUT" on her locker door.

Apparently several boys on the football team got word that "she'd tried to blackmail" the football coach, and the team was up in arms to defend their great leader.

It escalated. The faculty and PTA got involved. Jane stopped going to school. The coach and his team kept up with practice as usual.

The president of the PTA took interest (God knows what insight she had—probably her own experience with a Dick) and worked to get Jane back in school. She sent Jane a bouquet of flowers with a card that read, "You were very brave to come forward."

After two agonizing weeks back at school—none of the students, male or female, would talk to her—then Jane opened her front door one evening, surprised to see the president of the PTA. She could only muster, "What do you want?"

"I want to help you…and the other girls at school." She had Jane's attention.

"Remember the card? I wrote that you were very brave. Well, you are and now everyone is going to know about it. Since you had the courage to come forward, four other young women have also come forward, with their parents. He did to them what he did to you. And worse. He has a long history of this. It wasn't your fault, and he won't ever be at the school again."

Lesson

Oh, Jane. This story is so sad and so common. This Dick comes in many friendly, helpful disguises: coach (swim team, gymnastics, soccer), troupe leader, neighbor, friends' male siblings, teachers, doctors and family members. The truth is, she's fortunate he didn't do worse to her.

There are many lessons to be learned in this story. As always, be wary of authority figures who offer "special help" all alone or activities with "just the two of you." This is the screeching of the circling eagle about which mother rabbits warn their bunnies. Run!

Second, *signs of resistance*? What 14-year-old, 80-pound girl caught unaware and paralyzed with shock can put up a fight against a goddamned football coach? She only got away without worse because he didn't force the issue. End of story. The sad truth is that most girls, even if they had a chance in hell of defending themselves, would be too horrified to think clearly and put up any defense whatsoever. Only someone highly trained in combat would know how to respond well in a situation like that—and even they might freeze up.

So once again we see evidence of the theme of our work. Women are left extremely vulnerable and ill-prepared to avoid or escape attacks from their predators.

"My kids know what to do. They talked about it at school."

Please! "Stranger Danger," my ass! This does absolutely nothing except leave parents and teachers thinking they've fulfilled their duty. Girls (and all children) need to be taught, reminded, given examples, drilled, role-played. Then do it all again. And again. That's real training. How long would a cat survive if its mother showed it a photo of a dog once or twice and said, "Doggie Danger!"

Janes everywhere, find the strength to stop hiding from the truth and to fulfill your duty! For almost every Jane attacked by a predator, you can trace back along her life story and find a woman who failed to warn and train her properly about her natural predator.

There is no way a 14-year-old girl should ever be alone with an adult male outside the family circle of trust. Period. Drunk Uncle Willy and your lecherous old grandfather are not in the circle. What decent man would want to put himself in that awkward, risky position if he had honest intentions? He wouldn't! But a Dick would.

An acquaintance reported to me that when she was 15, she was subjected to a "physical" at school. The girls were "tested" by a male doctor who had the girls lower the waistline of their pants so he could feel their lower abdomen and upper groin area. She felt strange about him touching her and the other girls there, but didn't know what to say. Then she heard the girl down the row—who'd already developed large breasts—say to the doctor, "But I don't want you to put your hand up my shirt." He insisted that he had to "listen to her heartbeat," and forced his hand up her shirt.

This behavior would be highly offensive, unexpected and punishable in many countries—and not just those ruled by extremists.

If young girls are taught to be modest and to protect themselves, but then are "officially" forced (through what *is*—but is not *called*—abuse) to expose themselves and to be touched by adults, the confusion and subsequent behavior—labeled "loose" or "slutty"—of many Janes is no surprise. They're doing as they were taught.

Parents of girls, and even boys, must beware of entrusting their children to strangers. Get a clue! Can they read? They need to buy a newspaper or pop online from time to time. Hello…altar boy? More like "fodder boy." Scout troop leader? A man you don't know is taking your kid into the woods overnight?

Adults are molested all the time, so what should we expect? It won't happen to our kids because they are "too young" to be looked at that way? Required reading, folks: one year's worth of news—and not just finance, sports and funnies. Plus counseling for living in denial.

Now back to Jane and the pigskin Dick. Courage. This guy was the town hero and Jane paid a heavy price going public with her attack. She was lucky not only that he didn't do worse; she's lucky that the truth was finally revealed with others coming forward.

First, let's talk about what to do if you are *in* this position with a Dick.

Fight, Jane! Scratch his eyes out. There are other self-defense techniques, and it's wise for all people to at least have basic training. But until you do, that one will help. Chances are, you won't actually scratch out his eyes, but you'll have a much better chance of getting away if you resist. Police say you have a tremendously better chance of getting away if you fight, fight hard and don't stop fighting! Resist! Never give up. Even if it happens, you'll know that you tried to defend yourself. The result is not as important as the effort. Did you show up with your best? That knowledge alone will help with the healing.

Whether fighting an attacker or doing dishes after breakfast—always bring your highest energy, Jane. It's one of the secrets that should be an integral part of our life training from our mothers.

Regardless of exactly what did or didn't transpire, go to the police the moment you escape. Don't hesitate. Don't wait a second.

Physical evidence will only be available immediately after the incident.

So, what to do if you have been abused by a Dick in the recent or even distant past?

Jane, if you're ever in this situation you have two legitimate choices. The first is the one I choose. Blow the whistle. Let it come down! Go nuclear! If they did this to you, do you know what that means? They did it to others—and will continue until stopped. You may be the sacrificial lamb that suffers for going public with the facts, but *do* it. Save your sister Janes, and potential male victims, from this kind of predator Dick.

The other choice is one I discourage, but every Jane has her own life and choice. If you've been abused in any way by a Dick and just can't bring yourself to blow the whistle, do anything you can to protect yourself from him. I'll say it again, I recommend the nuclear button to protect future victims, but that's my personality and ability. If you can't do it, for God's sake, Jane, at least don't let it go on. It wasn't your fault, but now you should know how to protect yourself and prevent that shit. Surround yourself with love—there are so many wonderful people to spend your time with. Haul ass away from the Dicks of the world.

CHAPTER 5

THE WORST DICK OF ALL: FAMILY DICK

There are few things worse than betrayal by those we have reason to trust. And the greatest pain and betrayal is perpetrated on people who believe they are loved and protected by the perpetrator, those too young to understand or to defend themselves—children.

In this chapter we will look at the some of the most challenging situations a woman (young and/or grown) can encounter in dealing with Dicks. Some of the characters in these stories belong in therapy, some in a hospital, and some behind bars. But since all too often they're in our homes and roaming free, we need guidelines for confronting them—and support as we deal with their offenses.

The ideas presented here and throughout this book are just that—ideas. Every woman needs to find her own path, her own strength, and her own support for freeing herself physically and emotionally from family Dicks.

If one reader finds a way to free herself from a family Dick, the pain I suffered as a child from family Dicks will have been transmuted to good. If you free yourself or help and inspire another to do the same…we'll slowly but surely build a safer, more beautiful world. Onward and upward, Jane!

Black Diamond Dick

A woman in Colorado was dating a man whom she deciphered correctly was a Dick. She had several reasons to believe so, and decided she would rather walk the path alone than with a fool. Several months after she broke off the short and not sweet relationship with Dick, her two younger brothers and the man she was dating at the time were killed in a car accident. Our young Jane was devastated. She didn't eat or sleep for days and didn't leave the house for several months, except to run errands and work.

Slowly, she began to accept invitations and mix at social events. A neighbor invited her to a Bible study group and she decided to go. Guess who she runs into at the first meeting? She's in mourning and highly vulnerable, so there he is, ready to pounce—the Dick she'd dumped almost two years earlier. He offers to give her a few free ski lessons, and within ten months they were married.

The Worst Dick of All: Family Dick

He was earning about $1,500 a month as a part-time ski instructor and she was earning about the same as a waitress. But he had a plan.

He said he knew it might be painful for her to part with them, but the four paintings her brother had left her in his estate were appraised at almost $10,000 a piece. He'd recently met an art dealer from New York—yea, the guy taking private ski lessons—and he said he could take them off their hands. Then Dick could start that business he told her about, the one he'd always dreamed of.

She was a generous woman and the idea of holding anything back from her husband was unthinkable. What was hers was his. Of course he could sell the paintings.

"Good, I thought you'd say that, which is why I already sold them before he went back to New York!" he beamed like the cat that just caught the bird.

Did you hear that, Jane? It was a strange sound you may not recognize if you live in the city. It's the sound made by the screech owl mere seconds before it swoops down on a field mouse or bunny.

She wasn't angry for what he'd done. And though it wasn't her motive, she benefited richly from it. Dick took the money, built a wagon and hitched it to a shooting star. The construction industry in Colorado had just started to move out of a seven-year slump, the tiny village they lived in became a booming ski destination and they were millionaires almost overnight. Dick's company was so successful, in fact, that he had numerous managers running things for him and he had ample free time. For skiing, like before, you wonder? Keep reading and we'll find out.

About three years into the marriage, with a two-year-old by her side and a six-month-old in the carriage, Jane received a phone call from a stranger to inform her of her mother's death.

"My mother's death?" she repeated, thinking the caller must have the wrong number. "My mother passed away 10 years ago."

The caller shared more details, but this served to further confuse Jane. "Oh, my mother-in-law? But my mother-in-law also died years ago."

She hung up the phone and called her husband's cell phone immediately. His voice revealed that there was a long story, something she wouldn't like, but he only said, "I'll come home early tonight. We'll talk about it."

Feeling nauseous and sensing that something was very wrong (uh, like, *duh!*), the distraught wife drove to her husband's office. He wasn't there, and the manager said he thought she might find him at the ski lodge. And so she did, tucked away by the fireplace drinking hot toddies with a woman he uncomfortably introduced as "an old ski student."

As the evening unraveled there by the fireplace, the old student made a dash for the door, the husband sought to minimize the damage, and our poor Jane's life as she knew it began to disintegrate.

Dick succeeded in smoothing things over, for the moment. He explained that he'd always told people his parents were dead because to him, they were. She knew some of the stories of his childhood, and wasn't that enough to understand why he would do that?

Oh, why was he at the lodge instead of work? Well, when she called to tell him the news he just needed to get out for a breath of fresh air and a drink.

The student? Uh, she'd just walked by two minutes before you arrived and sat down to say hi.

Jane was consoled, but only because she wanted to be—unable to deal yet with what the truth would mean for her.

Weeks later she couldn't shake the gnawing sensation in her stomach and decided a heart-to-heart conversation with someone would help. She decided to call her new friend who worked at the mountain bike store not far from the lodge.

"Sorry to bother you, Gina, but I'm so upset about my husband and have to talk to someone." Before she could say that it was because his parents had been alive all the while he pretended they weren't, Gina jumped in.

"You *and* his ex! She was in here the other day looking for him and she was pissed."

"What ex? I didn't know he had any ex-girlfriends living here?"

Then the other ski boot dropped. "Not his ex-girlfriend. His ex-wife."

After a few moments of silence, realizing that the charade was going to end anyway, Gina decided to elucidate for our sweet simp.

"God, you don't know anything, do you? Yes, he was married before. Well, maybe it doesn't really count as married because she had it annulled after she caught him at the pool with another woman while on their honeymoon in Vegas. I never felt it my place to say anything before, so I didn't bring it up, but he's legendary for sleeping with half the skiers on the slopes and—I'm really sorry to be the one to tell you, you seem so sweet—but you should know. That hasn't changed since you got married."

Jane did what any woman in her shoes would do at that point. She called an attorney and filed for divorce. And how did Dick respond? He had a coming-to-Jesus experience. Just like Saul, a bolt of truth struck his ass right off his skis and he saw the light. He was shamed by the error of his ways, and was ready to be a new man, a true man, a *family* man!

"Let's go back to Bible study—it's where we found each other again and it's where we can renew our love and commitment!" he begged.

Jane, do you know how this story ends? Here it is, and please fasten your seat belts. She took him back; and he used the next year to read everything from Genesis to Revelations, and to hide the assets from his now multimillion dollar business before he filed for divorce and left her to marry his "old student."

Lesson

Understanding the lessons of this story will prove more valuable than an Ivy League degree in making your life a richer experience. Jane was a sweet woman doing her best to keep her family together. But all her sweet efforts amounted to nothing but wasted energy in the end, as it goes with such things. She could have spent that loving energy and generosity on someone worthy.

Taoist Master Hua Ching Ni in his book, *Moonlight in the Dark Night*, says that caring for such a man is like caring for a tree that will never give fruit. And so it was, but it could have been avoided. But how?

Oh, we all know the answer already? Then how come we've all been in this position, in some twisted form or nasty fashion, during our lives? We know, and yet we still get ourselves in trouble. We refuse to see what we know is there. *We lie to ourselves.*

Many of us could have seen the first sign. Most of us would have known by the second. A few Janes may take as long as this sad Jane to realize that her Dick was the walking pestilence! But did she perhaps recognize that something was off right from the start?

What was her first reaction to this man? No, not when they saw each other in Bible study; the first time. Correct, she thought he was a Dick and she left. Women could so often spare themselves heartbreak if they only *believed in themselves and stopped trying to pretend what they want is there when it's not.* She knew!

When hearing the roar in the bush, the gazelle doesn't wait to see the lion before running.
–ALLIE CHEE

But then what happened? When she was in a weak point in her life, he reappeared. It could have been any other Dick as well. We've already discussed this, but, Lo! Let us repeat it 10,000 times and yet 10,000 times again if necessary. Do not make life-long commitments or huge changes while in a time of healing. Heal first! You say you're just coming out of mourning and think it might be the right time?

After you take a cast off a broken leg, do you run a marathon the next week? First therapy. Then walk gently. Slowly build the strength, then run, and then train for the marathon.

Even if she had missed her first internal message about this Dick, if she had moved more slowly, his true character might have revealed itself before her life was entangled so deeply in the muck of his existence.

> *When you want to test the depths of a stream, don't use both feet.*
> **–CHINESE PROVERB**

We won't count the painting episode as one of the major warnings, though it should be. Even when partners are generous and share everything with one another, they still extend the respect of asking or discussing before doing something like that. You ate my last protein bar without asking—cool. You sold my deceased brother's paintings left to me in his will without asking—you Dick!

> *Even the hand of compassion is stung when it strokes the scorpion.*
> **–PERSIAN PROVERB**

So finally, she had her third chance. Undoubtedly, this was the most difficult, because now there were children to consider. Was her discovery that of a loving husband's weak moment in which he made a vacant-minded decision? Had he lied to her about something trivial, simply trying to avoid a fight after a long day's work? Those things can happen in a relationship, and people must determine for themselves if their partner, and thus their relationship, is a house built on a quality foundation with a small crack—or if it's a McMansion built on a landfill near the San Andreas fault.

However, when you have numerous examples of decades of deceptive, destructive behavior, it's time to pull up and flee with all haste. It's not time for further energy depletion (called discussing it, fighting, hating).

It's also not time for therapy, marriage counseling or looking the other way. Just time to leave—without hesitation, and if possible, without wasting words. If, when walking on a trail, you encounter a snake, are you going to stick around to see if you can work it out and make each other happy? You see the snake, you hear the rattle—*haul ass!*

What about the house and the business?

Let the court decide that.

What about the kids?

If he is a decent father and there's nothing to prove the contrary (unfortunately, being a lousy husband and having a despicable character—in other words, being a Dick—doesn't legally qualify as a bad dad), then no court in the world would prevent him from seeing them. Whether Jane likes the idea of it or not, they will still have a father if he wants to be there. If you leave, they'll still have two parents—with *just one* living a lie, instead of two.

Dirty Old Dick (Back to the local pharmacy)

New Years Day! That meant time for BBQ and football at Grandpa Dick's "summer camp" in Arizona. There were cabins, and children from around the country came to stay in summer to learn archery, horseback riding, hunting, fishing and swimming, plus ride dirt bikes, horses and jet skis.

Jane didn't really get along with her husband's family, but he seemed to love hanging out with them so much, she went along without too much resistance. She could never really figure out if he loved Grandpa Dick for his Dicky self, or the fact that he was an old mega-millionaire with few likely heirs.

BBQ smoke, buckets of beer bottles and a lively crowd greeted them. Jane and her husband, Dick Jr., made their way to the poker game going on in the family room where Grandpa Dick presided.

"I always quit while I'm ahead!" he slammed down his cards to give a big bear hug to the new arrivals.

"Who's up for some swimming in the pond?"

"We're still playing poker."

"It's cold."

"We're gonna eat."

"Well, I've never seen such a group of sissies in my life. "You!" He pointed to Jane's kids. "I bet you're too citified to want to go swim in an ole green pond!"

"We're in!" responded Jane's son, 11, and daughter, 13.

"I'll go, too," Jane chimed in reluctantly.

"Naw, you stay here. You'd just ruin that fancy manicure."

Jane, relieved to be off the hook, sat down with Dick, Jr. to watch the game on TV.

"It's getting dark," Jane said to her husband. "Should they still be swimming?"

As they approached the pier, it was difficult to see, but it looked like they were already out of the pond and Grandpa Dick was helping the kids dry off.

As they approached, Jane stopped, frozen, as she saw that Grandpa Dick was indeed rubbing a towel over their bodies—their naked bodies.

"What in God's name?" she yelled.

"Aw, the kids wanted to do a little skinny dipping, country-style. I didn't see any harm in letting them."

"They what?" Jane asked, knowing it was a lie and looking at her husband for support.

Dick, Jr. silently looked back and forth between his wife, his father and his children.

"Kids, that was a strange thing to do. From now on, wear your suits—even in the country!"

The Worst Dick of All: Family Dick

Grandpa Dick excused himself to get back to the game.

"Mom, we didn't want to skinny-dip. Grandpa Dick made us," the daughter sobbed.

Jane snapped at her husband, but before she could say anything he turned to his daughter and said, "Aw, it's not really important who thought of the idea. Just don't do it again."

On the drive home, no one said a word. After the kids were in bed, Jane closed her bedroom door and raged at her husband.

"What the hell? You let that man, your father, do such a thing… my God…I say 'such a thing' and we don't even know exactly what he did…we didn't even ask them! Whatever it was, we know it was sick. You let him do whatever he did without a word?"

"Well, I was surprised by it just like you and wanted to get out of there to think."

"Think about what?"

"About how I'm gonna kick that dirty old pig to Kingdom Come," he hissed.

After a fitful night's sleep, Jane waited to hear how Dick, Jr. was going to deal with his father. Strangely, he said nothing about it. Not all day.

Next evening she asked how he was going to handle it. He snapped, "I'll handle it." End of the story. She never heard more on the subject, because he never did anything. However, they did stop socializing with that side of the family so at least she and their kids didn't have to see Grandpa Dick.

One year later, the week before New Year's, Jane asked her husband what they should do for the holiday.

He looked at her as if she were daft. "Go to Grandpa Dick's. Like always. Whole family's gonna be there."

Lesson

Jesus H. Christ! Who's the worse Dick in the story? It starts out with Grandpa Dick, the quintessential old pervert molester who should have been castrated, branded and put out to pasture years ago. Yes, years ago, because there is no way these two young kids were the first. And because of Jane and Dick, Jr.'s cowardice, they were most certainly not the last. They were undoubtedly two in a very long chain.

Now, on to the other horrible Dick in this story—Dick, Jr. What kind of man can witness such a thing and do nothing? An accomplice. That he's more concerned about protecting his inheritance than his children makes him an equal offender.

> *Who can protest an injustice and does not is an accomplice to the act.*
> **–THE TALMUD**

And Jane! WTF? Frozen by insecurity and fear? A mother's first job is to protect. Remember our animal friends. No mother rat would intentionally lead her little ones into a trap. If Jane behaves like a huge number of women in this position, I bet she took them to Grandpa Dick's house this last New Year's Day for a BBQ. And God knows what else. Let's pray for them.

We women must, must, MUST find the strength to protect our young—no matter who the predator. Failing to do so is not only a crime of law and spirit, but it places us lower on the maternal plane than rats.

Brutus Dick

Jane and her sister were born near Mexico City. They were two of seven siblings, all of whom slept on the floor around their parent's bed "like little *perritos*," Jane explained. They ate beans and tortillas sparingly all week and looked forward to Sundays. That was the day their father went to market with his weekly paycheck and they prepared a feast: all the beans, tortillas and salsa they could eat.

While sitting in the living room of her five-bedroom Spanish revival home in the hills of Los Angeles 20 years later, Jane spoke longingly of those Sundays as a child.

Jane had it good—but she'd earned it with pain many people could not endure. Hers was a remarkable story of those who sacrifice everything to reach *El Norte* and a better life.

The Worst Dick of All: Family Dick

Things had not gone so well for her sister, Bertha. Lacking discipline and resolve, the only thing she'd created in the U.S. were offspring whom she didn't have the means to support or the wisdom to care for.

Since her first border crossing, Jane had sacrificed for her entire family. She visited her parents, making several trips a year to Mexico with suitcases loaded with *dólares* to assure her parents comfort and security in their old age.

Jane's now deceased parents left five siblings who'd remained in Mexico and took freely and ungratefully of her generosity. They grew to expect—and even demand—the support she gave lovingly. Always working, planning and caring for others, Jane ignored many of her own needs, including her hopes of being a mother.

No surprise then that when Bertha showed up on Jane's doorstep, two little boys and a howling baby girl in tow, Jane opened her heart and hearth.

"I'll pay rent, *hermana*. *Te prometo!*" Bertha said.

It didn't take long for the hurricane that was Bertha's life to blow through Jane's house and rip asunder her hard-earned tranquility. It started with a foreboding breeze.

One of Bertha's boys threw a baseball through the sliding glass door.

Jane's dog chewed an old suitcase of Bertha's and Bertha demanded a new one.

The maid quit because Bertha had physically threatened her for "stealing" from her purse. Bertha demanded that Jane reimburse the hundred dollars. And the rent she was going to pay?

The hurricane occasionally built to a Category 3, then dropped back to a base level tropical storm.

Late in the evening, Jane and her husband Dick would lie in bed and discuss what to do.

"She's got her issues," Dick said, "but she's going through a lot. Give her some time."

Jane appreciated Dick's patience and understanding. If he hadn't been cool-headed, there was more than one instance when she would have thrown her sister out on the street.

Dick was a landscaper who spent most of his days outside and away from the house. That's why when Jane returned home in the middle of the day (having finished a big job ahead of schedule), she was surprised to see Dick's truck in the driveway.

The Worst Dick of All: Family Dick

We interrupt this program with an emergency broadcast. Hurricane Bertha, barreling over hot waters, is now a Category 5. Residents valuing their health and sanity are advised to evacuate immediately.

She walked in the house to find the three kids planted in front of the TV. "Bertha? Dick? Anyone home?" She searched for them room by room. She heard something in her bedroom closet and followed the…moaning sounds?

Que puto! Que puta! What's Jane to do in that position? I'll tell you what she did and it's exactly what I would suggest, with a few exceptions. She kicked out that Dick and *bruha* sibling.

But, she still gave Bertha money to set up an apartment with her kids. *For cryin' out loud, Jane! Cut the umbilical cord with this cucaracha.*

Lesson

Some might say that Jane gave Bertha the money for the benefit of the children and not her. To those who do, heed these words of wisdom: People who grow accustomed to grinding sympathy and support from others because of their self-created problems and addictions will suck you dry—all to no real benefit. Love them, wish them well, send them packing and change your locks and your phone number. When they begin to help themselves, that's when you can step back in with more support.

The "husband," that *pinche verga*. The last I heard he was sporadically showing up at AA meetings, unemployed and suffering miserably for the wife and life he'd lost.

We all have to make our own decisions when confronted with a Dick and betrayal of this magnitude. My answer, after years of work, leaves me with this approach:

You're a loving, positive relative or acquaintance =
You're in my life and I treat you like family.

You're a negative, hateful relative or acquaintance =
You're not in my life.

But I do lovingly wish you all the best…and one other thing… Lose my address.

Do not take revenge, my friends, but leave room for God's wrath, for it is written: "It is mine to avenge; I will repay," says the Lord. On the contrary: If your enemy is hungry, feed him; if he is thirsty, give him something to drink. In doing this, you will heap burning coals on his [Dick] head. Do not be overcome by evil, but overcome evil with good.
–ROMANS 12:17-21, NIV

Granted, this quote is a little scary—*heap burning coals on his head?* Was the writer having an off day while channeling the Divine? Nevertheless, it's just a creepy way of saying, "conserve your energy." Words of wisdom, indeed.

When you've been betrayed by a Dick to whom you've given your all, this quote is more comforting than mom's homemade stew and hot chocolate by a warm fire.

Keep it on your fridge.

Royal Dick

Jane lived on the Cape with her wealthy parents in a home that was the envy of even their blue-blooded neighbors. Servants were abundant and she had a stable of polo ponies she trained and raised. Though her parents were both good to her, there was constant friction between them, and Jane could sense her parents' growing problems.

As a young adult, it became dreadfully clear that her father was having affairs. She'd even noticed with gross discomfort the long gazes and over-friendly greetings her father gave her girlfriends when they came to visit. This dramatic shift was more challenging for Jane, but it was the '70s anyway and, at 19, she could relate, if only slightly, to the idea of an open marriage.

One day returning from a neighbor's she heard unprecedented shouts and commotion in their otherwise staid home environment. Screaming came from the living room where she found her mother, father, one of the servants and the servant's 14-year-old daughter, Aisha. "Don't deny it!" the servant glared at Jane's father, pointing to her daughter's belly. "My girl's pregnant and your husband did it. You going to jail, mister. You going to pay for this—heavy!"

The Worst Dick of All: Family Dick

For years Dick had been sleeping with the servants, and now one of the servant's young teenage daughters was pregnant.

Her father! The man who taught her to ride a polo pony, who took her on cruise ships to London and tours through the Mediterranean. The man who entertained senators and governors in their family rose gardens.

The threat of charges had been dropped—Dick had made it clear that his money could either be enjoyed by the servant and her daughter or used in court to prove that the servants had stolen his wife's jewelry. With the promise of $100,000 cash or assured jail time, what would anyone do—even the mother whose daughter had been raped by her employer? She wasn't the first woman in the world to be abused and have no form of protection. There are mocha-skinned people all over the South to prove it. (Just a little historical fact, y'all—everybody stay cool.)

Jane confronted her father. "You had affairs. Fine. But how could you sleep with such a *little girl* and get her pregnant?"

"I didn't think she was old enough to get pregnant or I would have been more careful!"

"That's your answer? Your defense? You raped a girl and got her pregnant because you though *she wasn't old enough to get pregnant?*"

This story ended as the majority of stories end in which the perpetrator of a tremendous crime is in the family. Everyone swept it under the imported, 10-million-knot silk rug and played the family game. The loving and neglected Mrs. finally divorced that crazy Dick, but not until she'd watched him move the servant, her daughter and his newborn son into the guest house to "make right" what he did.

The daughter? She remained friends with her dad, albeit with a cool distance.

Lesson

Jane, listen closely. Come a little closer so you're sure to get it. Are you listening? That was a vicious, violent crime against a minor, Jane. If you know about a crime and do nothing (even if it's your family), some folks—and the law in many places—would say that makes you an accomplice.

How would the ending have differed if the rapist had been the guy who does the lawn and Jane had been the victim? Would someone *then* call the police? Would someone press charges and protect further victims from this violent criminal? The answer is obviously yes. But when it's a husband, father, uncle, brother, son who commits the crime against a female family member or friend, what happens? People sink deep into a pitiful state of illness and denial, pretending it didn't happen.

In my travels and studies around the world, I have found this phenomenon everywhere. A friend of mine from Iran told me incest in her country is so common and unpunished, it's simply called, "Using What's Yours." (It's not more common in Iran than anywhere else, but that way of expressing it left an indelible impression.)

Are only those people from underprivileged neighborhoods, ghettos and the like supposed to go to jail for violent crimes? Jane, this situation calls for the deepest and strongest sense of honor— and the toughest of tough love. If you would call the cops if it were a stranger who committed the crime, you simply can't allow the criminal to run free to harm others if he's a family member. Do what is necessary to put Dicks of this magnitude where they belong: in jail or in a hospital where they won't harm others.

This reminds me of a story written by a Native American medicine man about healing from physical sickness, but included an episode of an elder medicine woman being asked what to do in the case where a young tribesman had raped one of the women. "Throw his body from the cliff. If he does have a spirit, it will be free," she said.

Without addressing whether or not it is the correct solution, for a conversation about capital punishment, that's a thought-provoking way to express it. The deliberation is not about incarceration or other punishment, but about *liberation* for the spirit of the criminal—if he has one.

Back to our time and place. The world is positively teeming with wonderful, loving, healthy men. So why is it that almost every woman we know—and many men (who actually find the courage to speak about it)—have been abused or violated in some way by a Dick?

It's because Dicks on the loose get to 5, 50, 250 men, women and children over the course of their lives because none of the victims or family witnesses/accomplices find the courage to stop them, leaving criminals running wild for years. If there are only 10 Dicks on the loose in a small town, over time that could mean 500 victims. This is, of course, why we read headlines about a lone priest raping 500 altar boys over a 30-year period; a schoolteacher who molested dozens of children; and…you see the point.

If the criminal Dick is someone you love, you can still love them. You can forgive them. But don't leave them on the loose.

If a sick or injured bear were running loose in a campground, would you set up the tent and gather around the fire with your kids, or would you call animal control? You have the power to protect countless people. Find the strength, Jane.

"When we forgive evil we do not excuse it, we do not tolerate it, we do not smother it. We look the evil full in the face, call it what it is, let its horror shock and stun and enrage us, and only then do we forgive it.'
–LEWIS SMEDES

From "Forgiveness—The Power to Change the Past,"
Christianity Today, (1/7/83)
[And remember to call the cops.]

Lit-Up Dick

Jane, at 25, had five children. Her village was a seven-hour walk from the end of the closest bus stop connecting to Lima. Life there didn't offer many opportunities. The only abundance was kids, alcohol and corn.

Her children had grown up hearing their father roar. Dick almost always had a bottle with him, and the more he drank, the louder he roared. He usually left the children alone, his anger vented on his wife with a single theme: He was sure she was having an affair, though she wasn't.

One night when Dick came home late and Jane was cleaning dishes from dinner, he insisted that she'd been out sleeping with a neighbor that day. He grabbed her by the hair and dragged her into the street, forcing her through the village, pointing at the different houses, "Was it with him? Huh? You *puta*, who was it? I'll kill him."

By the time the children ranged from 5 to 14, the violence had escalated from verbal abuse and threats to beatings. They didn't believe their mother when she would explain away wounds with stories of her clumsiness.

After listening to her mother scream several nights in a row, Juanita, the oldest whispered, "Is anybody else awake?" One by one her two brothers and two sisters expressed their fear of the violence in the next room.

"I'm telling you all now. The day is coming when I will make him stop!" Juanita vowed.

Two years past after Juanita's midnight vow. The violence came and went, mainly depending on how much work their father found, and how much money he spent on alcohol instead of food for the family. But then a team of archaeologists came to town—a group of 20 Europeans, mainly men, who set up camp on the path that led straight to the family's front step.

The father became obsessed with the idea that his wife was sleeping with one, maybe more, of the archaeologists. He flew in the kitchen into a rage, ranting about her infidelities of the day. Jane, who'd taken beatings silently for years, responded for the first time.

"Maybe I should. Maybe they would pay for food for your children."

His fury exploded. *Saltado* flew, dishes were broken and Jane took a hard beating. That evening Juanita made her decision and told her brothers and sisters her plan, to which they all agreed. They waited until both parents were in their bedroom. Juanita grabbed the gun she'd borrowed from a friend months before in anticipation of this night.

The five children burst through the bedroom door as a team, Juanita in the lead, gun held ready. She pointed it at her father. "We love you, both of you. But, Dad, if you ever touch her again, we've all agreed that the right thing to do is to kill you, and I will do it. Tonight is your only warning."

Are you ready to believe what happened next? If anyone ever tells you miracles don't happen, read this story to them. Juanita herself told it to me in a tent in the Black Forest in Germany years ago. That father, from that day forward, never hit the bottle or his wife again, and he and the children developed a decent relationship.

Lesson

While this story is incredibly intense and certainly not the ideal way of dealing with a Dick, one can't judge these children for the way they handled their situation. They lived in a village high in the Andes—how do we know what help they had available for addressing family violence? Yet here in the U.S., and in most big cities around the world, there are several options available to help stop a violent Dick from abusing his spouse or children. We Janes don't have to wrestle with weaponry—we just have to find the courage to pick up the phone.

A step toward a safe, healthy life is three buttons away: 9-1-1.

IDS (Irritable Dick Syndrome)

Jane was 18 and Dick was 20 when they married in the early '60s, when marriage at that age was still common in the U.S. Cruising rapidly down that common path, they popped out two boys in the first four years of their marriage. And then it started.

Dick was not prepared to be a husband—and he most certainly was not interested in being a father. The problem was that he didn't discover this little quirk until after he'd sired two offspring.

Jane grew up in a home that served up all forms of abuse and neglect so, in her book, Dick was a decent man. It didn't bother her too much that he left for work as early as possible. When he returned home well after the family dinnertime, he'd skulk into the kitchen, eat a loaf a white bread and drink a two-liter bottle of Dr. Pepper, then hide behind a book until he fell asleep.

Shoot! That wasn't so bad either. That was actually pretty good in Jane's mind: the money was tight, but nobody was molested and the bills were paid. Jane's only disappointment in the marriage was that she'd always wanted to have a girl.

The thing that most irritated Dick was any noise issuing from the children. Crying at any time irritated him. Crying at night, or early in the morning, or when he was watching a football game sent him over the edge. He'd spring from his recliner, yell a few obscenities and flee to his room behind his books.

His nerves are just shattered from that hard job he's got, Jane thought, and kids do make an awful amount of noise. Jane learned how to whisk the children away to their room when Dick returned from work.

The boys never heard affectionate words or felt comforting embraces from their father. But a phrase they knew well was, "I'm gettin' my belt!" which preceded the only physical contact they ever had with him.

Jane would continue cooking in the kitchen or cleaning her bathroom as if she couldn't hear her boys' screams. Somehow, she was never in the same room when he would unleash his fury. She never discussed or acknowledged the wounds as she changed their clothes. She and the boys could almost believe that she didn't know it was happening—and that belief was the only lifeboat the boys had.

When the boys were 7 and 5, a miracle occurred!

Dick became a decent human being? No, no. Dick sired yet another child and this time, hallelujah, *it was a girl!*

Life with a newborn in the house went on as usual, literally. When baby Tina would cry, Dick would grab his belt and beat... *the boys*. Anytime Tina woke in the middle of the night, the boys would lie in terror in their room, sometimes wetting their bed in anticipation of their father's arrival.

Yes, there were challenges, but Jane was happy. Dick had climbed the ladder at work (exactly as she'd thought—he'd been working himself to death and that's why he couldn't take the noise), money was abundant now and her favorite activity was shopping for frilly dresses and dolls for Tina—a new one every week for Sunday church. The ladies there fussed over her beautiful baby girl, so she always carried Tina into the main sanctuary rather than leave her in childcare. While Sunday was Jane's favorite day of the week, Saturday was the boys' most dreaded because Dick was neither at work nor at church.

As the years passed, Dick did mellow. The scowl remained on his face, his overbearing anger and lack of love were ever present, but he retired his belt. What happened with Tina? Nope, she was never showered with cuddly affection by her father, but like his wife, Dick took a special liking to his precious little girl. She was spoiled and spared, but she lived as a witness to the mental and physical violence doled out on her older brothers.

Lesson

Whose wounds and whose crimes should we tend to first?

Jane is pathetic. We acknowledge she suffered in childhood, but wouldn't that be more reason to protect her kids? Obviously. But more often than not, it doesn't work that way. She's like every other Jane who allows the Dick she chose to abuse her children. I feel deeply for this type of character. There must be incredible suffering in living with the pain of abuse in childhood and then the guilt of allowing it to happen to your own children—an unenviable life. We can feel immense disappointment and compassion for this character.

But in the end, we can't care how much Jane was abused. We can't care how tight money is. We care about protecting children and confining Dicks.

Look at an animal we consider lowest in nature. Let's look again at the rat, for an example. Rats care for and protect their young. Look at mother birds that risk their lives protecting their eggs from bigger birds of prey. How about the mother lion that risks her life to fight off the stronger male if he approaches their cubs? (I've seen that one on the Nature Channel and I would take a lioness as a mother any day. What a role model!)

Snap out of your self-indulgent fear and pity, Jane. Using old wounds to justify turning a blind eye to abuse is how the demons of fear, anger and abuse are passed down the generations.

The neighbor's dog bites your kid, you have it "put down." The neighbor bites your kid, you call the cops. Your husband bites your kid, you go paint your nails? Our first job as a mother is to protect the children. **First job—*protect.***

- You admit that you need help. Good first step. Now seek help.
- You tried to get Dick to go to counseling and he wouldn't go. That means he doesn't want to change. You have to change…addresses! Leave him. Protect your kids. He can still be in their lives in supervised visitations (if he actually wants to be).
- You'll have to go get a job as a waitress if you leave him? Tough shit. Go be a waitress and live in a dumpy apartment. Children would rather live in a tiny, dirty place and wear socks with holes than live with an abuser.

You're scared? Everyone's scared. Get help. Call a hotline or dial those three magical numbers— 9-1-1—if you don't know what else to do.

We're done with Jane, so now, on to the really tricky one. What about Tina?

What do we do with a girl who was loved and cared for, who in turn dotes on her parents even as an adult, and who's never called her parents to the carpet in defense of her brothers? Remember, life is sweet when we wish love and abundance for all our brothers and sisters on Earth. And we do wish that for her. But she's a chickenshit! She's the only one in the story (aside from the abuser) who wasn't abused. She should be able to clearly see (or at least a little better) all the dynamics and sift through the insanity. She could have intervened, even if only as an adult. I can't say exactly what she or anyone else should do, but it shouldn't be *nothing*, and I know what I'd do.

"Mom, Dad, you were wonderful to me. But you made me witness the horrible abuse of my brothers whom I also love. For hurting them and making me watch, you've never acknowledged or apologized. Until you make it right with them, it's not right with me. I love you, and I'll wait for your call—if you decide to make it—to tell me what you intend to do about this."

Not everyone can or should respond like me, but to brush it under the rug—terrible.

Air that dirty laundry, Jane. Blow the whistles and sound the alarms. Blunt honesty and openness. A wound smothered in bandages festers. A wound out in the sunlight heals.

Do it, Jane!

And now it's time to move on...

PART 2

Part 1 of this book was about knowing when, why and how to *run*.

Some people are born with innate talents, and one of mine was *running!*

I grew up in Texas and did have some beautiful experiences, but not one family member was someone with whom I was safe or happy, other than the other children my age. My cousins and I were like war buddies—serving as shields for one another in the crossfire. And we all came away with battle scars. Growing up in that kind of environment generally does one of two things to a person. They succumb to and are possessed by the demons—passing them on to future generations and allowing their lives to crumble. Or they find a way to rise up and out of those conditions—a journey that can last a lifetime.

I chose #2.

By God, I rose up out of my childhood, running with two pistols blazing: one aimed toward the past and one toward the future. I was going to shake anything from the past I didn't like and claim anything I wanted from the future.

At 23 I made what I now jokingly call my "Great Escape from Texas." I set my sights on Laguna Beach, CA, to start a new life—strapped with college debt, no savings and a job from a generous friend who'd said, "I'm starting a new biz and can't pay you anything—it's commission only—but you can live in the spare bedroom here with my wife and me for free till you get on your feet." Despite the amazing benefits package, I hesitated.

Shortly after I received that offer, I received a package from a friend who lived in Huntington Beach, CA. The box had no card, no explanation—just a little iridescent clay bowl containing a handful of sand and a shell. I held the bowl in my hand for about an hour, then gently placed it on my nightstand. I opened the bedroom window of my cheap 1970s apartment and yelled at the top of my lungs, "I'm moving to California!"

Within two weeks, the arrangements were made and the car was packed. On the big morning I was to commence the drive on I-10 West, I walked out of my apartment door and looked in the parking lot with horror. During the night, someone had hit my car—badly.

I was about to fall on the sidewalk and start crying, but then I pulled out those two pistols. I thought, "Nothing can stop me that easily. If this thing still runs, I'm outta here—on schedule."

I entered my car from the passenger door since the driver's door was too damaged to open. I put the key in the ignition, turned it on and put the car in reverse. I listened for strange sounds. Nothing? California or bust!

I experienced enormous change after that move. I began to love my life in Laguna, but there was something missing—and I didn't know what.

It was then that I had a unique experience with Mother Teresa that I referred to at the beginning of this book. Forgive me if you've read my book *FREE LOVE: Everyday Ideas for Joyful Living*, but this Texas gal is telling the story again here.

In 1993, I experienced something new and fantastic that I'd never known: freedom from fear about my ability to pay the rent and the joy of being able to buy—within reason—any food, dwelling, car, clothing, jewelry or vacation that I desired.

I'd been working since I was 13. I worked my way through college, holding down two and even three jobs at a time. For the first time in about a decade, I had only one job (albeit a challenging one), no homework and cash.

Party time!

Or so I thought.

I was living in Laguna Beach, I had a few good friends and life *should have* felt pretty good. But when I read *The Bridges of Madison County*, the best-selling book of the day, I burst out crying and didn't stop for two days.

I remember lying on my futon, swollen eyes, throwing empty Kleenex boxes into a pile of tear-stained tissues strewn across the floor. The book struck a chord with a lot of people—it sold 50 million copies—and that was pre-Internet. But crying for two days and going through box after box of Kleenex? I knew I was dealing with something more than this book. *Why?* I was from Texas and I might shed a tear or two in private if someone passed on…but bawl like a baby over a little story?

For me, it was the story of a woman who'd accepted what was supposed to be "a good life," did what she believed was "right," but had not followed her heart's desire. The message to me was: You can have passion, travel and excitement *or* the love and security of family—but not both. I don't know if I'd see it that way now—it's been 20 years since I read it—but that's the way I saw it then. I realized it struck a chord because not only was I not following my heart, I didn't even *know* where it wanted to go. Like so many people living as "transplants" in our country, I felt a serious lack of family, community and love.

I started a journey of inner exploration and, over the following weeks, I came to this conclusion:

I loved Laguna, I enjoyed making lots of money and I loved my friends. But I didn't feel deep love or a sense of belonging in my life. Likely we all come to this conclusion at some point—or points—in our lives. When we do, we either hide in our work and busyness—or we start exploring, thinking and praying, trying to find meaning. This process is called *soul searching*. This was my time.

When we're in survival mode and busy beyond belief, we don't have time to dally with soul searching. Like being caught in the surf, we can't pause to enjoy the view of the horizon while we're trying to get through the next wave and maintain our breath. But once we break through the surf to calm, open water, we can pause for perspective.

It didn't take much soul searching for me to conclude that I'd made many decisions merely in the name of survival and financial gain and that my heart was lonely and longing. I was in love with work and travel. I wanted to see the world. I was also missing meaningful relationships. Maybe I had to accept that I couldn't have both. I decided that the only way to find true meaning and love was to set aside my personal passions and "give love away." But to whom?

My friends in Laguna had families and lifelong friends. Of course I could be a part of their lives, but those relationships couldn't go to the depths I wanted—at least not in a few months or even a few years. I wasn't in communication with my family—for healthy reasons—and wasn't about to look there. (There's been a lot of healing and love in the family since that time.)

Lying on the beach one day, it hit me: *I'm going to Calcutta to work with Mother Teresa!*

(Random, but not as random as it might appear. I went to Catholic school and had even decided—in second grade—to be a nun when I grew up. I gave up that idea after praying under a tree, expecting the Virgin Mary to appear as she had in the movie they showed us at my school. She no-showed.)

That evening I went home and called Mother Teresa. I called again and again. I don't know how many tries it took before I got a line through, but eventually I got to her. (India has come a *long* way in telecommunications since the early '90s.)

I spoke with her on the phone, as with an old friend, for about an hour.

Only one hour with Mother Teresa changed the direction of my life forever.

She asked me why I wanted to come work with her, and I told her. This is what she told me:

"To learn to love is the most difficult and important thing we do."

"Your first job is to learn to love yourself. Many people fail to ever do this."

"Your next job is also very difficult—and only if you succeed in the first—and it is to learn to love your family."

"And then your next job, if and only if you succeed in the first two, is to learn to love your neighbors. Pick any neighbor, get to know them, care for them and love them."

"And then, finally, if you've learned these three things—that would be a good time to identify strangers who could use your help. You said you live in the Los Angeles area? I imagine there are one or two needy people there. But if you still want to come work with me in India, there are always more people here who need help than those who are willing to help, and you will be welcome."

Hmmm—what I needed was exactly what I had thought I needed—a lot of love in my life. And now I had an outline of how to go about giving, receiving and *living it*.

Mother Teresa, a wise and loving mother.

Go, Jane!

She gave me many gifts in that call. She taught me that I didn't have to turn my back on the things I loved, the places I enjoyed or the pursuit of financial gain to find my sense of belonging and true love in life. She taught me that I could find it anywhere I was, or anywhere I chose to be. She set me on a path of learning to give and receive love—which led me around the world and back—several times. And to countless wonderful experiences I'd never dreamed of.

That brief moment with Mother Teresa, and traveling the world and finding so many people to love and learn from, changed my life and formed the basis of the ideas in this and all my writing. I began a lifelong journey of learning to love. I'd always been a pro at "run." Now I wanted to be a pro at "love!"

But, as we know now, if we're entangled in a life with a Dick, the flow of love is cut off. That is why we learned to run in Part 1.

> *"You never change something by fighting the existing reality. To change something, build a new model that makes the existing model obsolete."*
> **–BUCKMINSTER FULLER**

After reading Part 1: *Run, Jane!*, we should know better how to identify, free ourselves from, and preferably *avoid* Dicks. We

The Worst Dick of All: Family Dick

identified and addressed a deep gap in our personal development and the way young girls are raised and how this affects almost all women at some point in their lives. We were not taught (or taught well enough) how to identify and avoid our primary predator: Dicks. But now we know what to do and how to do it!

Now that we've been through the material in Part 1, we should never need to read that part of the book, nor experience those things in our lives again.[6]

We should also open the windows, burn some incense and say a prayer of gratitude to clear the air in our dwellings or wherever we are right now.

Reading that material and experiencing the emotions it triggers is tough stuff. It's important to have done so. We can't ignore those topics, pretending they don't exist. Every female has lived one or many of the stories in Part 1—and their daughters, nieces, cousins and grandkids will, too, unless we learn how to teach our children the lessons we have learned.

---

6   Obviously, many of us will need to work with family, friends and/or professionals to continue to move away from and heal our spirits from experiences addressed in Part 1. But as I've said, my role in this book is to provide the loving swift kick in the pants to help all Janes make a break from those situations and patterns, and to encourage Janes to take the first step.

Now it's time in this book and in your life to separate completely from those themes and that energy. We've learned how to *run*. Now it's time to *stop!* And time to learn to love.

It's time to put away our middle finger and to use our hands—and lives—for what they're intended, as I first learned in my hour with Mother Teresa: loving ourselves; caring for family, friends and community; and creating beauty.

Since I myself am still learning, and since we're all on different paths, I'll just offer a few ideas that have been helpful for me in learning to live in love. You'll find these ideas beneficial, and maybe they'll inspire your own original ideas.

CHAPTER 6

BEYOND PREDATOR AND PREY

To move beyond the "predator and prey" mode of existence, we must remain vigilant and constantly pay attention to our choices to see that they are congruent. There are countless proverbs and sayings about congruency:

- Like attracts like.
- Birds of a feather flock together.
- Water seeks its level.
- Show me your friends and I'll tell you who you are.
- Lie down with dogs, wake up with fleas.

If you love your relationships and are having positive experiences, then you're on the right track. Keep doing what you're doing. If not, there's only one answer: You're not making congruent choices and you're in conflict with yourself—which can only lead to conflict with others.

When you have clear ideas about who you are and the way you see your life going, you must be constantly watchful that your actions and choices reflect those desires. Anything else is just a detour wasting your own and other people's time. Of course, life is full of detours; that's how we learn. However, the more we do that leads to what we don't want, the better we know what to do going forward—by remaining vigilant and focusing on congruent choices.

Here's an analogy to help demonstrate the point:

Cali Or Bust

If you live in a two-horse town in Texas, and you really want to live on the beach in California (sound familiar?), make sure that your every effort leads West. New York might be a fun side trip, but it takes you thousands of miles off course. Do you really want to delay your move that much? Hawaii might be beautiful, but didn't you decide that you wanted to move to California more than anything? Don't take detours, no pit stops in Vegas along the way. It's Cali or bust.

Applying the analogy to relationships: If you want a serious relationship that will lead to marriage and children, date men who want a family.

If you say: "But, but, but...!"

I'll say:

- He gets freaked out when you say you're looking for marriage? Good! He saved you a lot of both time and energy with his honesty, so you won't go on a long detour to Miami.
- He's single and wants to date around? Good for him. Don't try to be the one to change his mind. Let someone else—who also just wants to play—play with him in Reno while you keep heading west.
- He's in the middle of a divorce. Oh, that's a detour to a ghost town. There's nothing there you want to see and it's on the other side of the planet.
- He's married. That detour has horrible potholes and a steep drop-off at the end of an unmarked road. Stay on I-10 to Cali and get where you *really* want to go.

Even if you stay your course, life will take you off track. You'll run out of gas along the way. You'll read the map incorrectly. You'll have people you thought trustworthy give you wrong directions and take you off course briefly. But stay focused and you'll get there.

What if, in the end, you never make it as far as the beach, but land in Palm Desert? Life isn't about getting exactly what we

Go, Jane!

wanted anyway; it's about staying true to our vision—and thus ourselves—making congruent decisions and dying knowing that we showed up consciously and followed our dreams.

That leads to another analogy. All my friends have heard the one about…

The Eagle And The Pigeon

You believe (at least I hope you believe) that you have all the qualities of an eagle. You are strong, beautiful, independent and noble. You fly high. You certainly don't consider yourself a pigeon: a common thing. You aren't like the millions, pecking away at the ground for scraps and dumping poo-poo in everyone's path. So far, so good.

The only problem with being an eagle is that they're rare beings. If you're going to take the high road, you want people in your life who are also on the high road. *They are out there*, but be aware that they're harder to find. Thus the great challenge for an eagle: periods of deep loneliness.

If, during your loneliness, you decide to fly down and play with the pigeons because it's better than being alone, you won't be the first. Just know that if by chance another eagle flies by and sees you in the gutter scraping for a crust of bread, you'll be mistaken for a pigeon and the eagle will fly by.

An eagle waddling on the ground with a pigeon is incongruent. The look is different; the activities are different; the energy is different.

When the activities, look and energy of the people with whom you spend your time are congruent with your desires for your life, you will feel more than good. There will be a deep peace and you will know that you're where you should be. If you fall into great conflict, constant heartbreak, huge drama—check out your surroundings.

Since I love metaphors, I have a few more:

You Can't Change Your Friends, so Change Friends

Don't worry about the people with whom you're spending your time. First, you can't change people or carry them to an energy level that *you* find appropriate or desire.

Have you ever heard the expression: You can't change friends, so change friends? When you raise your energy, the change happens automatically. The people resonating at a different level than you disappear from the scene—either you show them the door or they find the exit on their own—either way, happy come, happy go. On the spiritual plane, we're all brothers and sisters, so you will wish they go forth and prosper. On the experiential plane, there are many brothers and sisters for whom we feel love, but in our daily life, they need not exist.

A Fish Lives In A Pond
(or, If You Want a Fish, Don't Go Looking in a Tree)

Don't worry about where you'll find a man nor spend time "fishing" for him.

The worst example of this is women who claim they're looking for a nice, conservative boyfriend, but troll nightclubs full of wanna-be porn and rock-n-roll stars drinking and doing drugs. Yes, a few people in those environments might also be looking to build a nice family, but there are places where there's a more congruent match and greater possibility of meeting like-minded people. Remember the expression: A fish lives in a pond. If you like fish, spend time in ponds! If you're looking for a nice, conservative Jewish family man, the odds are better you'll find him in activities at your local JCC or synagogue (a pond)—not partying in a bar at 2:00 AM or at the craps table in Vegas (trees).

Your life changes the moment you make a new, congruent and committed decision.
–ANTHONY ROBBINS

But even while spending time in ponds, you're doing so because it's an "energy match" for what you like and the way you like to spend time—you're not doing it to hunt down your guy.

Even in a pond, continue to focus on yourself. Raise your energy. Deepen your spirituality. Do the things you love and spend your time in activities and an environment that is congruent with what you want for your life—*and, yes, in a partner.*

Then, at the right time, there he'll be. Life, even in our greatest moments of doubt, truly works that way, whether we believe it or not. If you're busy doing what you love, even something as simple as shopping at your local farmers market—and then accidently lock yourself out of your car—there he'll be in the parking lot, a "Slim Jim" in hand and ripe for a soul mate.

When we live in congruency, not only do we improve our health—mind, body and spirit—but we also move beyond "predator and prey" scenarios. The predators simply fade to black. They don't exist for us. And if one happens to slip into our vicinity, we now know how to give them the shake.

CHAPTER 7

CHILL, JANE!

In ancient North African cultures, wandering away from home—literally wandering in the desert—was considered the greatest education, and essential for moving with strength and confidence into adulthood.

There are few people who would argue that travel, new experiences and activities—all the things we collectively call "broadening our horizons"—is counter to personal growth. However, when it comes to relationships, having numerous, multicultural, diverse experiences leads to great things—and a significant challenge.

If you've only lived in a trailer park, then a trailer park is what you know. If you grew up in a dingy trailer park with rusty trailer homes, then your vision of beauty might be a trailer park with mowed grass and clean, new trailers. However, if you leave that trailer park and see homes, gardens, even castles around the world, would you ever find a trailer park beautiful again? Reminiscent of home, yes. Cozy and comforting, maybe. But beautiful, never.

And so it is with relationships.

Everyone knows that as we get older, we get more set in our ways. What I'm suggesting is that it's not just that we get set in our ways—that's true, but it's more complex than that. Once we leave our "trailer park" of inexperience, we desire more and more—and in the case of a partner—qualities. Expectations can become excessive—which can lead to disappointment and create problems where they are none.

If you've had more than three decent relationships, you can reflect back and instantly think of a single word that you associate with each man:

- He made me laugh—and it turned me on!
- He was so kind-hearted—and I was enchanted with him!
- He was so intelligent—and I admired him!

And on and on.

We love the unique qualities in each person. And then we want these qualities in the next person. Each new person is greeted with an ever-greater challenge to be what we find "perfect." The first one was funny, so now we want funny. The second one was giving, so now we want funny *and* giving. The third one was brilliant… you see the point. If you're 35+ and single, your next poor man has to be the funny, smart, muscular, wealthy, spiritual, devoted—*the Don Juan you always wanted.*

How can any one person ever live up to collective experiences we've had and qualities we desire? If he can't, sometimes we mistakenly label and treat him as a Dick. In writing this book and speaking with hundreds of people about relationships, one of the first responses I heard from every man was, "Hey, we're always labeled a 'Dick' if we're not tough enough *and* sensitive enough; affectionate enough, but giving enough space—how are we supposed to be 'enough' of everything?"

When He's Tom or Harry, Not Dick

Slow down, Jane! If he's not superman, it doesn't mean he's a Dick. Your job is to determine from your life experiences the most important quality or qualities you want in your partner. Then make congruent choices, letting go of your other needs and expectations.

In other words, we can't throw around the name "Dick!" Save that for when it truly applies.

He might be a slob; he might be broke; he might be careless or insensitive at times—but that doesn't make him a Dick. If the men in your life aren't perfect, but aren't Dicks, chill, Jane! They may not be the friend, partner or boss for you, but we don't want to use this name for people living with positive intentions. We've got others to reserve it for, those who have done a lot to earn the title!

I used to be a Dick—until I grew my balls.

–A REFORMED DICK

CHAPTER 8

BEING YOUR OWN BEST FRIEND

There is no friendship, no love, like that of a parent for a child.

–HENRY WARD BEECHER

It's an aberration of nature that occurs frequently in the human species: people failing to be loving parents and friends with their children. A more extreme aberration: parents who are outright Dicks.

If our parents were one of these aberrations, it is terribly painful and difficult to overcome.

But…*good news!* As Dr. Wayne Dyer says, "It's never too late to have a happy childhood!"

How is that achieved?

In the end, no matter what has occurred in your life that you perceive as negative (encounters with Dicks and others), the answer EVERY TIME (after you've extricated yourself) is to focus with all your energy on *self-cultivation*—which is an expression of *self-love*.

Self-cultivation helps you to be the partner you're looking for… and the best friend you're looking for.

What is self-cultivation? It is the process of literally raising your energy: mind, body and spirit. There are lofty heights to be reached where whatever occurs cannot affect you negatively—but in the interim, there is salvation and peace in the process itself.

Everybody will find their own road to friendship and peace with their internal life, but here are a few ideas.

Questions to ask about previous low-energy experiences:

1) Am I at peace about how I handled the situation?
2) If not, is there anything I can do now to make myself feel better about it, and to further protect myself and other potential victims?

3) In what ways can I use my experience to grow personally?
4) How can I use the lessons of this experience to help others?
5) What things can I do, starting immediately, to self-cultivate?

Here are some pointers for self-cultivation and *the action* of loving yourself, especially relating to our interactions, relationships and sex.

Forgiveness

Why is forgiveness a pointer for learning to love ourselves? Because the inability to forgive enslaves us (not the Dicks!), binding us in the shackles of bitter feelings. It tears down—not the Dick's health—but our health; and, worst of all, it limits our ability to love.

From my own experience, I believe we can *decide* to forgive, and *study* how to forgive—and those are necessary steps—but the *feeling, release and utter joy* of forgiveness comes when it comes. It may be short or long in coming, but when it does, there will be no doubt. It's as strong and clear as the feeling that sages describe when talking about "enlightenment." You'll be able to look back and say,

"There I was, sitting on my deck. It was a cold morning and I was drinking tea, reading about X, when suddenly it hit me out of nowhere like a bolt of lightning. I put down my book, looked out at the hills and I knew I was done with it. The anger was gone. I just wished them love and let it go."

And, even more exciting, when you've really reached this point, "it" (the anger, fear, disappointment) may come back in small ways, prompted by little reminders, but it will never own you again, making it easy to return to the love and letting-go.

Forgiveness is all-powerful. Forgiveness heals all ills.
–CATHERINE PONDER

Energy Gardening

Energy in the garden of your life is choked off by weeds. Restore the positive energy flow in your life by weeding out all sources of negativity. Your perception of what is negative will be personal, and it will change as you raise your energy. If you view your life as a garden, it's easy to understand—cultivate yourself as you would a garden. Plant beautiful things in an artful way, give them nourishment and care and constantly tend to the weeds lest they choke out your flowers.

What are "the weeds?"

In the world of Traditional Chinese Medicine, pregnant women and even women wanting to conceive are advised to avoid listening, viewing or engaging in any activity where there are violent, hateful images or speech. If it's beneficial for a new life, it's probably a good idea for a mature life, too. Consider the violent or hateful images you take in.

For some people, avoiding violence might simply mean avoiding violent, R-rated movies. For a more delicate spirit, it might include shows, books, movies, friends or any household with frequent quarrels and displays of low-energy: intoxication, bickering, pettiness, sexual behavior and social conduct that violates one's personal code of behavior. Even much of what we call "comedy" is full of negativity and violence. Unfortunately, by being hyper-exposed, we are desensitized.

If you eliminate salt from your diet for only two weeks (which means you would have to prepare everything from scratch at home—no cans, boxes, bottled sauces or dressing), you would first experience salt-withdrawal symptoms. Food would seem boring, and your appetite would initially increase with cravings and then decrease with the boredom. But on the 15th day, you might double-over when taking a bite of any processed or restaurant food. All you would taste is salt, though only two weeks earlier you might have thought your favorite foods didn't have any salt added unless you had added it yourself. So it is with exposure to negativity.

Make a list of every source of negativity in your life and how you'll weed it out. It might include a few items such as:

- My sister Suzy. Her friends and family have bailed her out of a bad marriage and financial woes more than a few times. Till she stops drinking, seeks some form of regular counseling and gets a job—no loans, no lunches. Love from afar.
- My friend Carol gossips and lies. Everyone knows that the one who gossips *with* you will gossip *about* you. We've had some good times, but time to love her from a distance and lose her number.
- The guy I'm dating speaks disparagingly about women every time we're together. Neeext.
- My neighbor down the street hates dogs and everyone who likes them. Avoid walking by his house.
- Any TV show in which the subject, even if presented in a "humorous" way, is gossip, revenge, cheating, violence. Change channels or read an inspiring book.

- Any radio, news or web program that encourages feelings of anxiety, hate or fear. Put on my own playlist.
- The Dick who works in the cubicle next to mine. Find a way to communicate as little as possible with him. If that doesn't do the trick, determine the next step.
- Myself! Focus on love, peace and prosperity. Know that I will encounter negative people and situations, and it's up to me to maintain my internal harmony. Which leads us to...

Guard Your Mind As You Would A 3 Year Old

Our mind, untrained and unleashed, will terrorize not only those around us, but itself—meaning *ourselves!* Observe your thoughts. When you find yourself dwelling on anything in the past that you perceive as negative, make a shift. Quote an affirmation, say a prayer, repeat a positive mantra—anything to cut off the pattern and eliminate it.

Some schools of thought claim it is helpful—rather than trying to stuff down or "replace" a recurring negative thought—to charge a negative thought head-on. Ask your mind for the source, the real fear and reason behind the thought, and see what feedback you give yourself. If it's a thought or fear that's been difficult to shake, this is something to consider.

The neurons in the brain responsible for communicating our thoughts make connections with one another just like new roads are built to join old highways and open new patterns of transportation. Eventually, these roads in the brain are established, so the thoughts can motor through your head on cruise control.

If you are unable to eliminate unhealthy or worrisome thoughts, there are spiritual and health professionals who can offer additional help. Look for resources to support you on your journey.

Get Out Of Your Head

Didn't she just say to guard our mind at all times?

Yes. And sometimes, when you find your mind running in circles, bemoaning the unfairness of life, wallowing or feeling down, one of the most immediate cures is to "get out of your head." Stop thinking about yourself entirely.

How is that possible?

One way that works for me is to think of someone else—someone in real need of help or love. Make a few calls to tell people you love them, prepare a special meal for someone, volunteer your time in a charitable organization. Doing something for someone else is often the best thing we can do for ourselves.

But not just anyone…

Beware The Tar Baby

You know the story. You're skipping down the street, whistling a tune along with the sparrows and there it is: the tar baby, sitting on a fence and looking adorable, needing your help. You hold out your hand and, *hmm*, that's strange; it's stuck on the tar baby. You use your other hand to pry it off, and, *oh, my!* Both hands are stuck. Further attempts to free yourself further complicate things until, *good grief!* You're completely entangled with the tar baby and there's no way to get unstuck.

We've all had our share of run-ins with tar babies. Sometimes the tar baby comes in the form of an alcoholic who keeps promising to stop (but needs a few thousand bucks to get a fresh start again). Sometimes it's the sweet, sunny personality who just can't keep a job, and jeez, can he crash on your sofa for a few days? He has an interview at a new restaurant that's opening at the end of the month. Sometimes it's the pathetic family member who tries to make her self-created agony everyone else's problem emotionally, financially—or, most often, both.

There is only one thing to do with a tar baby. Love them from afar—way, Way, WAY afar! Don't commiserate with them. Don't give them money. Don't load your back with their burdens. Ideally, don't even take their phone calls until they show some sign of being engaged in their own healing.

All the help, money and time you invest in a tar baby is energy down the drain. Help people who are working to help themselves. The people who throw their hands in the air, blame the world for their woes and expect you to fix it (then are ungrateful and turn on you like a scorpion when you cut it off) are tar babies.

In short, when you're skipping down a path, gazing at the butterflies and smelling the roses, if you see a tar baby put their hand out for help…avoid them as you would the plague. That frees you to give energy and love to yourself—and to friends and those in your community who are also seeking to live in love.

Choose Your Battles

We've all heard this metaphor and it's one that merits review. Even in a peaceful life you will be presented with a constant flow of situations and encounters. And you can navigate smoothly or turn them into battles. Sometimes—but rarely—it's appropriate to do battle. In a common, 24-hour period, these situations can arise:

- Your alarm doesn't go off and you wake up late.
- The kids didn't clean their room last night.
- You're out of eggs, which you planned to make for breakfast.
- Your man left for work without taking out the trash or making the bed as he said he would.
- You spill your tea in the car backing out of the driveway.
- Since you arrived late to work, the boss makes a snide comment and gives you a dirty look, which he does with frequency whether or not you're late.
- Your neighbor calls and says she saw your boyfriend getting warm and cozy with another woman in a café last night.

So how can we approach such a day and maintain internal and external harmony?

- You're up late; you can't change that. Call work, tell them to expect you at 9:00 rather than 8:00 and that you'll stay late. Then peacefully go on about your morning. You can't control how they'll react at work—that's their choice or battle. You can't undo waking up late; it is what it is. Be cool.
- No need to get angry or yell at the kids. Explain calmly that since they ignored your request to clean their room, they will clean it this evening before enjoying dinner. And since they failed to listen last night, they also get to sweep the backyard as well.
- You're out of eggs. Smile. It's time for oatmeal.
- Your messy man—he's forgotten before and he'll forget again. Either take the 10 minutes to make the bed and take out the trash with a smile on your face, or leave it as is and put a smile on your face.
- You spilled your tea. No biggie. It dries.
- The boss gives you a dirty look. That's cool. Smile back and get to work.
- Now on to your neighbor's call. Is it time for battle? As always, Jane, stay cool. It could be a mistake. Always remember: There are people who thrive on stirring up trouble where none exists. Maybe it wasn't him. But then again, maybe it was. While remaining calm and cool, get to the truth of the matter and handle it in a way that conserves your energy and minimizes the time you remain in a state

of disharmony. There may be a peaceful resolution once you determine the neighbor was wrong. Or it may be time to engage in a battle—but even then, it can be approached in a way that speeds your return to a state of balance and peace.

This exercise may seem redundant or obvious, but since so many of us know these things yet don't *live* them, it's worth the moment to review them—*again and again*. Focus your efforts and energy on the things that matter—the good and the unpleasant, too, as long as they really matter and can be changed. It's important to discriminate. Don't exhaust your energy (a.k.a. life force) on things that can't be changed, or on nonsense, irritants and turds.

The less we focus our energy on battles, the more energy we have to focus on love. And the more we live in love, the fewer battles we have. See the circle?

Don't Be A Nutcracker
(Not to be confused with a ball-buster)

If you try to crack every nut that crosses your path and work to wrestle every tiny bit of nut out of each shell, you're going to be a busy, miserable little squirrel. So what's a nut?

A nut isn't someone who's necessarily a Dick—he just can't give what you want.

Let's look at a few examples.

Jane was dating Dick. He was 35 years old, never been married, no kids, beautiful, intelligent, liked by all—and to top it off—he worked with *handicapped children*. Seemingly, a perfect catch! What woman 25-40 wouldn't drool? They all did, and he never did. Until he met Jane.

No one could believe how much time Dick and Jane spent together. His friends repeatedly said they'd never seen him *so* in love, that he'd never spent so much time with any woman. "He said he loves you and wants to have kids with you—and he *never* says that about *anyone!*"

Beware, Jane! Could he be a tough nut to crack and you—and only you—have the right cracker? Maybe, but proceed with caution. If a man 30+ years old is still reputed for his inability to be in relationship past the first month, if he's never said he loved anyone and says he *never* wants to be married or have kids, don't be enticed by the challenge to be the one who cracks that nut.

I can hear it already.

But he's never met anyone like me.

Is that so? You're a great person and *you* took him in. Think there haven't been other nice people who took him in? There were. You are special. But so are the others. If he hasn't found anyone in 30 years with whom he can spend more than four weeks, spell it out with me: I.S.S.U.E.S.

A person who can't receive love has no love to give. We can wish them well and be friends with them, but nothing more. If he can't move into the deeper, more intimate levels of a relationship by age 30, *whew!* Girl, you really don't want to be the one to crack that nut. It will be a lot of work—10 years for every one it normally takes to know someone, and the path will be extra steep and nasty. Better to leave him to revel in his reputation as the one who never falls in love, who can never be caught and go shower your love on someone who can receive it and has love to give.

You Lay The Card, You Play The Card

When playing cards, it's best to know the rules before you start. One of them is: Hold your cards until you're ready. Then, if you lay a card down on the table, that's the one you're playing and you don't get to pick it back up or change cards.

Here are a few examples from life's card games:

- You start flirting with the boss—you laid the card. He's going to take his turn now and what card is he going to play? If he lays his card and you like it, you'll call it "flirting back." If you don't like the card he plays, you may call it "sexual harassment." If he chooses to fold and not play with you, you may call it "unemployed."
- You tell your landlord, Dick, that he can replace the toilet handle that broke six months ago or you're moving—you've laid a card. If the next card he plays is to *not* make the improvements, you'd better be ready to move.

Here's one of the most important cards a woman can play—and playing it incorrectly can damage lives and create mountains of regret. Put down this book, go turn off the music, close your door—and return to reading with all your focus.

It's called the *safe sex card!*

In a perfect world, a man and woman have the "discussion" *before* they have sex—and not just 60 seconds before, or worse, not until it's too late. They discuss birth control methods, VD testing, VD control methods and if, in the instance that their chosen form of birth control fails, they decide together if they will opt for an abortion or raise the child together in or outside of living together. Finally, I may need to mention, in that perfect world, they are both *honest*.

- If you have herpes, he has the right to know ahead of time if he wants to risk contracting it by sleeping with you—and vice versa.
- If you are the type of person who would absolutely never get an abortion, that should be discussed.
- If you never want to have kids and would most definitely get an abortion, he has a right to know.
- If, after reading the full *back page* of the advertisements for contraception in the magazines (with a magnifying glass and a PhD in biomedical sciences), you believe the types available for women are detrimental to health, then he must know ahead of time and agree to be responsible with condom use and/or other methods of birth control. (FYI: The World Health Organization has listed several forms of oral contraceptives and estrogen replacement therapy as carcinogens.[7] *Study, Jane!* And make educated decisions.)
- If he'd rather bust rocks in a chain gang than have kids (and will move overseas to impregnate underage girls who

---

7 http://gerardnadal.com/2012/02/15/world-health-organization-data-on-birth-control-pill-and-estrogen-replacement-carcinogenicity/, 11/15/12

have no recourse if *you* end up pregnant), you have a right to know.
- If he doesn't plan on giving you a dime, now or ever, for an abortion or child support, you have a right to know.

Now, back to the real world. I'm going to tell you what your momma should have told you.

This discussion is not intended for mature, loving couples in committed relationships. It's for all other sexual encounters: casual sex, people who are dating or people who for some reason have gotten themselves stuck in a relationship with a Dick.

If you have not carefully followed the outline above before you have sex, and there's a consequence—a price to be paid—*you* will pay. You may pay the price even if you followed the "discussion" outline above. If he stays and is loving, that's as it should be. If he shares expenses, that's the right thing. If you don't get VD, count your blessings. But allow me to repeat boldly:

You're playing with fire if you expect you can lay that baby-making card and then believe there's no chance that you'll have to play that card by yourself.

That's the way nature made us, sisters. We're the ones in which the child grows—and crying "injustice" is like stomping your feet and pouting to stop a thunderstorm. Is it unfair? Maybe. Does it suck? Sometimes. Are there laws to protect mothers? Yes, but what do they protect? Maybe you can pry a few bucks (and sometimes women pry a few million, but that's a different subject) out of the guy…and?

What about the man who agrees to coitus interruptus ("pulling out"), and then is sloppy and gets you pregnant. Sometimes it is effective, but here's a saying about that form of birth control that would be smart to keep in mind:

Sex is like basketball. The guy dribbles before he shoots.

Knowing that, you should then know that if you get pregnant, *you* got yourself pregnant. You can't count on someone else to protect you. I'm not saying it's fair. Again, it's just the way it is.

What if he's really loving, you're planning to get married *and* he botches the coitus interruptus and you get pregnant. Hopefully, it works out the way you'd planned, but if it doesn't, well, back to nature—the baby grows in the female and that child is your responsibility.

Jane, if you agree to be the one responsible for contraception and the man has sex with you thinking you cannot conceive, you bear the burden and the result is entirely your responsibility. If you use your contraception faithfully and still get pregnant (very rare, of course), it's unfortunate, but this is your problem.

Hold on, Jane! I'm not saying he shouldn't be involved in the resulting pregnancy, but I'm helping you navigate the real and beautiful jungle of life, not Fantasy Island. If he's involved, that's often the best scenario for you, him and baby. If not, you were warned ahead of time by Allie Chee!

That's the way it is, so accept it and use it to make decisions that leave a wake of beauty behind you rather than a wake of emotional destruction. We should strive with joy and discipline to conceive when it is safe, healthy, a mutual choice and the child has at least a chance of two loving parents working in unison.[8] Even with the best of intentions, it doesn't always happen that way—that's why there are 6 billion of us instead of 1 million—hee, hee! And, hey, that's OK. It's the way it is. But we can build even happier lives if we make better decisions.

There are instances—those involving she-Dicks—where it's not Dick who's created a less-than-ideal situation with parenthood. We won't go into it in detail since I know it doesn't apply to

---

8   I'm obviously working on the premise that a child with one devoted, loving mother and one devoted, loving father working together as a family—as in the way nature/our biology set it up—is ideal and what I'd wish for every child. However, the way it so often occurs doesn't resemble this set-up at all. The adults who raise a child can include single parents, steps, adoptive, gay and lesbian, and other combinations. From what I've seen in 44 years—for kids raised in these different scenarios, the odds are about even that they end up as healthy and happy (or not) as those with a biological mom and dad at home.

any of my readers. But there are women who, either through being sloppy with their birth control or through an intentional "robbing" of sperm, become pregnant while insisting they were protected.

Would those ladies knock over a bank? Would they hot-wire a car? How low can they go? Damn, they must knock 'em dead at parties with their limbo!

You can spare yourself and all the innocent bystanders (including the progeny) tons of misery if you remember the simple rule: You lay the card, you play the card—so play your cards right!

Lots of things can be undone, but remember the ones that can't—and like Granny said:

Be good, and if you can't be good, at least be careful.

Which leads us to our next, special chapter…

CHAPTER 9

SPECIAL CHAPTER ON INTERNET DATING

Why a "special chapter?"

This is a subject that is still new in the history of human courtship and little intelligent has been written about it. Further, about half the marriages and new babies you see today result from online dating—it's a huge phenomenon, it's here to stay and it's growing! Hence, a special subject deserving special attention.

There is not a young girl but what is more or less tempted by some unprincipled wretch who may have the reputation of a genteel, society man... Parents who desire to save their young daughter from a fate which is worse than death should endeavor by every means in their power to keep them from falling into traps...there are many good men, but not all are safe to an innocent, confiding young girl.
–RUTH SMYTHERS[9]
Marriage & Love: Real Advice from 1894

A few details have changed since 1894. We don't go to balls or dance halls wearing corsets and floor-length skirts to meet and mingle with the opposite sex. We don't have our parents (for the most part) guarding our "chastity and honor"—meaning keeping us virgins—until we're married. And, of course, many of the things considered "a fate worse than death" are now "no biggie" or even considered healthy and normal.

Aside from that, what has changed?

---

9   **Marriage & Love: Real Advice from 1894**, Ruth Smythers, Summersdale Publishers, 2008, 2009; Morris Book Publishing, LLC 2011, pages 21-22

Special Chapter on Internet Dating

Not a damn thing!

Those "unprincipled wretches" still abound. But instead of lurking around dance halls, they're surfing dating sites. Which, of course, is much, much easier, requiring far, far less skill and offering tenfold opportunities for deception.

How difficult do women make it for these wretches to "score" online? From what I gather—not very.

I've interviewed approximately 100 men and women, ages 21-56, who use online dating as their primary source for dates and meeting new people. Though many of the women have happy stories, they all seem to have their share of disappointing—if not horrible—stories to share.

I asked them all the same questions and, hearing the same answers, concluded that there is an obvious pattern to male and female behavior online. This might be obvious, but I wanted more evidence to back up my assumptions. (Naturally, some of the men had stories of she-Dicks to share, but they're not our topic here.)

The Women:

- They divulge *lots* of personal information. The most frequent lie they tell is regarding their age. The lame post older pictures of themselves (meaning from a time they were younger), and the despicable post pictures of *other* people (as if it were them).
- They will correspond with many people at the same time.
- They leap quickly on any "applicant" online who looks at all "cute" and whose profile indicates a fun, well-to-do guy.
- They readily accept that what the guy tells them online is true or factual.
- They quickly accept dates, meeting the applicants as quickly as a few days after they first began exchanging correspondence.
- They divulge where they live (their address) within the first date or two.
- Not all were looking for a long-term relationship or marriage, but none were out just to "get laid."
- Despite that, they have sex with many of the applicants, often in the first month or even week after meeting.
- They expect more to come of the relationship after having sex, and are frequently "surprised" or disappointed when he "just doesn't feel that connection" or doesn't call back.

- They get back online immediately after experiencing a bad date or disappointing encounter and repeat their exact pattern of behavior.

I'm sure it doesn't, but if any of that describes you, dear Jane, I'm going to guess that you've had your fair share of encounters with Dicks. Naturally. You're behaving in a way that is inviting—begging—them to come in.

The Men:

- They do not, generally, divulge the same amount of personal information. They lie about their age, income, marital/divorce status and more.
- They will correspond with *dozens* of people at the same time.
- They leap quickly on any applicant online who looks "easy" from the photos she posts or the things she writes. Pictures of women "partying" or "looking wasted" rank at the top of the list.
- They don't necessarily care if what the woman tells them online is true or factual—other than if they've used a deceptive photo showing themselves to be better looking than "the real thing."

- They quickly propose meeting with the anticipation of getting laid.
- Not all, but many are perfectly happy if all that comes of a meeting is a "lay."
- Not all, but many are perfectly comfortable having sex with multiple partners.

If Jane is looking only to get laid or for a no-obligation, open relationship, none of this is a concern. However, she still should be on-guard for characters online who are worse than unsavory, those who are downright dangerous.

For most women reading this book, I'm going to assume that you're not cruising the Internet looking to get laid. I'm working on the assumption that you're a strong, independent, loving woman, looking for friendship, perhaps a nice dating relationship and, if the time is right and the stars line up, a life partner and even to build a family.

If that is indeed you, get out your spiral notebook and highlighter—you're going to want to take notes and memorize this.

The more things change, the more they stay the same. The only thing that Internet dating has done to the scene that didn't exist in

1894 is that it's infinitely easier for Dicks to reach an enormous audience of unsuspecting women.

When meeting men online, there is no one "referring" them to you—meaning you weren't introduced by parents, neighbors, friends at work or church, or, or, or—so there's no way to validate anything about them or what they say. Other than *time*, that is (and perhaps some research).

If you don't believe me now, you can just read now and believe me later.

You must, Must, MUST move very slowly with Internet dating.

I'm going to give you some examples of how I approached Internet dating—and how I met several extremely kind, intelligent, healthy, successful, fun men with whom I am still friends.

Rule #1:

Never meet a man in the first week you correspond. I preferred to wait 1-2 months, speaking on the phone frequently during that time, getting to know each other and discovering if there was really any basis for a friendship. If they're genuinely interested, they'll stick around.

Rule #2:

Never allow a man to come to your place or meet at his place in the first month or two. If there's an exciting connection, meet once or twice a week around town in cafes, restaurants, museums, movie theaters—but not in bars or clubs. Even if you enjoy drinking, try to keep that to a minimum during this time. Again, if he's genuinely interested in you, he'll stick around. We're not being prohibitionists here—just realists. We all know what happens when new acquaintances with sexually charged energy are having a great time and drinking! Again, if sex is the point, drinking will help the cause. Otherwise, keep it to a minimum and stay sharp!

(A side note: If you think sex with a hot new date is sexy...just wait and see what it's like when you've become truly great friends, a real love is growing and the physical desire has been mounting for months! *July 4th, Baby!* Once the spirit is engaged, it's a whole new experience. More on this below.)

Rule #3:

Amazingly, this one never goes over well with Jane, but men responded very well to this: Tell them you are not going to have sex with them until you know if you're at least friends...which takes some time to discover.

Looking straight in his eye, I would tell a man on the first date:

> "I'm sure it's not your intention, but I want you to know that we will not be fooling around or having sex tonight—and not for a while. I like to know if I'm *at least friends* with the person I'm fooling around with, and especially sleeping with—and that takes time. I know many people who allow people who are practically strangers into their homes and bodies, while saying they don't know them well enough to give them the keys to their car or house. Well, not me."

Without fail, Janes will say to me, "Oh, no way. You don't do that, do you? That would freak them out or scare them off."

My only response to that is, "Good." For anyone who was scared off, that's what I wanted it to do. I'm not looking for "drive-thru" fun in my life, and if that's what they wanted, they can go back home, jump online and someone who will give it up is only a few clicks away.

I've known Janes who have had multiple bad experiences with online dating. Yet hearing my advice above, they shake their head and say, "No way. I'm not saying that to a guy on a first date," and off they go for their next round of being used.

Back to the conversation I have on the first date: How *do* guys respond? The few I spoke to on the phone for about two months and then said it to were pleasantly surprised. Some even seemed relieved. (Probably not "relieved" that they weren't getting sex right away, but relieved to find someone who was strong enough to say what she wanted, didn't want, and displayed self-respect rather than desperation.)

I'll say it again: Hear me now, believe me later. Just try this and see what happens. Of course, you have to follow through on the words—no matter how hot he is or how much fun you have in the early days together.

Online dating is here to stay—and that's great!

It's a wonderful tool, and for those who travel frequently, don't live in the towns where they grew up surrounded by hundreds of family members and friends who can introduce them to potential partners, or those who don't enjoy the usual "party" venues where people meet and hook up, it's a great way to meet compatible people.

I loved online dating. Of course, I met a few characters I didn't want to see again, but they weren't bad people—or at least they didn't have the opportunity to be bad *with me!*

A final recommendation is that you use dating sites that require *some effort* to join. A small monthly fee, a long questionnaire—

something that requires the slightest amount of time and financial commitment.

Why?

Think about it. How much time do we spend on writing a resume? Or even shopping for a pair of shoes? But we're going to sign up on a website to find a date or relationship *in just 5 minutes?*

Things that are quality...things not easily acquired...require effort. If it's just laying on the street for the plucking—whoa!—no, thanks.

That's not you!

You are a powerful, healthy woman looking for a powerful, healthy man. Powerful, healthy people are able and willing to put forth effort to achieve great things!

So when going online... put out, Jane!

Not sex!

Put out the effort to make online dating a wonderful experience that will lead to exciting, beautiful relationships.

CHAPTER 10

YOUR THING

I love asking people, "What's your thing?" to which they always respond, "What do you mean?"

I then say, "Your thing—*the thing*—that you love to do."

Often—far too often—people answer with something along the lines of, "Well, hmm, I guess I'd say I like to travel; to read; to watch football; hang out with my kids."

I then say, "No, not a list of things you enjoy. I mean YOUR THING. Family life or friends could be one of your things, but in this instance I mean the thing that you, alone, must do. The thing that is the ultimate expression of your personal joy, your *passion* with or without family, with or without friends. Doing "it" is what gets you through your hard times, defines your good times and you know you *must* do it—or were even *born* to do it."

Far too often the response is, "Oh, well, I'm not sure if I have that kind of thing."

Not having a thing—an activity that gives you deep joy and fulfillment—is probably responsible for at least half of the goofy experiences women have (same goes for men, but we're not talking about them here).

When we're experiencing a rough patch in a good relationship, are down in the dumps after a relationship has ended or when we've been without one too long, it's our *thing* that can keep us focused, raise our spirits and help us return to balance. Without it, we're much more likely to do "stupid things"—and y'all know what I'm talking about.

If you have your thing, you already understand this concept and it's probably been a longtime source of fun, happiness and something to return to over and over like a good friend or favorite place.

If you don't have a *thing*, you need to get one! No one can tell you what your thing is, and you may have to experiment with several things before you find it. If you ever thought, "I'd love to be a great chef," or "I always wanted to speak Portuguese," or "It would mean a life worth living if I volunteered for the Red Cross," or "Gee, I've always regretted not studying ballet when I was a kid—I loved to *watch* ballet, but we just couldn't afford the lessons," or whatever the story—that's a good place to start.

If we can involve our friends and family in our thing, that's even more fun, but it's not necessary. We were born alone, we'll die alone and everything in-between will be happier if we find the *thing* that gives us joy and makes us feel more in love with life—even when alone!

CHAPTER 11

DO A MAN-FAST!

Notice this chapter title isn't "Do a Man, Fast." It's "Do a Man-Fast!"

Several years ago I'd reached a point in my life where I was sure I was ready for the big commitment and family but, for some reason, I had been making mistakes. I mean, seriously goofy, ridiculous mistakes—spending time personally and professionally with people *very wrong* for me. It was a time in my life where I should have known "the rules" and how to deal with Dicks, but I was clearly in a weakened state, and that's not the time to engage in new relationships or make major decisions.

What would many people do in this situation?

Frantically and desperately continue in the storm, trying to right the ship while hunting down "the right guy" or right situation.

Remember our word "incongruent" and what happens when we act incongruently? I realized I was acting incongruently. I was responsible for attracting and engaging with people whose lifestyles and personalities were completely incongruent with my intentions and desires. I had to identify the reasons why and correct them before I continued.

When you know you've gone down the wrong path and you're lost, the first thing to do when you recognize it is *stop*. But then what? How to get on the right path?

I reflected on the situation and my actions and recalled:

- When Native American tribe members needed to clear and focus their minds—particularly when it came time for a hunt—they would fast.
- When people are ill and ready to detoxify their bodies, they fast.[10]
- When the ancient sages and prophets of the world were ready to receive and deliver great messages, they would first go to a cave, the desert, somewhere special—and fast.

So I decided to do a fast—a man-fast!

---

10 Considered to be healthy and cleansing in many schools of nutrition; to be undertaken under the care of a health professional; and not considered right for all people or conditions.

That's right.

For 90 days, I decided not to go on a date or spend time alone with a man.

> *If a [wo]man has nothing to eat,*
> *fasting is the most intelligent thing [s]he can do.*
> **–HERMAN HESSE**

I'd never done such a thing (at least not intentionally) and was fascinated with how it would feel and what would transpire. I knew I wouldn't feel lonely, because I'd gone many times in my life more than 90 days without a relationship and I've learned over the years to feel happy hanging out with my best friend—myself. But I hadn't gone 90 days intentionally disallowing the possibility. What would come of it?

A few weeks into the fast, a female friend and I went out one evening to one of the hot restaurants in town. It was packed and we were sitting at the bar waiting for our table. Lo and behold, a very attractive, well-dressed man started making his way toward us, smiling at me. I wasn't concerned—a deal's a deal, and I'd made a commitment to myself.

As he reached the bar, my friend started laughing and said to him, *"Don't even bother!"*

He laughed and asked, "What do you think I want?"

"Whatever you want with my friend you won't get it. She's doing a man-fast right now."

He was caught off guard and laughed like a boy. "OK," he said, looking at me, "what's a man-fast?"

I explained it, and he showed good-humored understanding for what I was trying to achieve. He asked, "Well, if you gave me your number, and we spoke on the phone now and then for the next 90 days instead of going on a date, would that 'man-snack' be allowed?"

Dang! Cute—and funny! But I didn't break.

I thanked him, took his number and said, "If you want to be friends now, you might still want to be friends at the end of my 90 days. I'll call you then and we'll see."

So what happened during the rest of the man-fast? As with any fast, initially it was difficult to control the thoughts about the item from which I was abstaining—men. I experienced little cravings and longings.

In doing a fast—of any kind—we're confronting our fears and weaknesses. We're challenging our ability to overcome or be controlled by those fears and desires. In the case of our time with men and relationships, the worst mistakes we make are due to fear (fear of being alone, of being unlovable, of never finding the right relationship) and, simply, loneliness. It's our nature to want to love and be loved, to want to give and receive affection, to have companionship and to have fun! Yet if we make decisions regarding those healthy, natural desires based on fear and loneliness, well, Part 1 showed us some of the mistakes that will result.

During my fast, as with any fast, the chattering of the mind and emotional desires subsided, and in their stead something new emerged—calm. I felt a stillness and confidence that I hadn't felt in a few years. I felt clarity and knowingness that all was well and as it should be. There was no need for seeking or grasping.

Now that's a place of strength from which clear, healthy decisions can be made!

When you've shaken the "need," you stop attracting the wrong characters and stop repelling people who are balanced and can sense when others are off-balance. You'll find yourself suddenly immersed in circles of wonderful friends and situations.

What happened with Billy (the man-snack)?

At the end of 90 days, I called him, and sure enough, we became great friends. We spoke on the phone as friends, then went to lunch as friends. We'd walk our dogs together in the creeks around town, trade stories about our families, work and dreams for the future.

What would have happened if, on that first night, we traded phone numbers with the intention of dating and exploring a sexual relationship? He was cute, funny and intelligent, and he thought I was. So we probably would have dated a while, and then later discovered all the ways we weren't a match for a love relationship. Then, since there would be hurt feelings and unfulfilled expectations, someone would break it off—followed by an awkward phase and a strong possibility that we wouldn't remain friends.

Isn't that how it happens all too often? Because we fail to approach the relationship correctly from the outset, we end up creating hurt feelings and "throwing away" wonderful people who could have become good, if not lifelong, friends.

As it turned out with my approach, we became such good friends so quickly, we never even bothered dating and finding out the hard way that we were an incongruent match for that kind of relationship. As a result, he's still my friend whom I get to love—a friendly love.

In a true love relationship, we can only have one partner[11] (some try for more, that's their prerogative), but we can have lots of friends. I'd love to have a whole posse of "Billys" in my life, and we can if we approach relationships with friendship in mind first—without clinging, grasping, jumping or longing for the perfect fit with every guy we meet and like.

As with all the ideas offered in this book—they're just ideas. You don't have to follow them or even like them. But hopefully you'll give them a try or they'll inspire your own ideas that bring you to more balance, deeper happiness and better relationships.

If you're in a good relationship and you've read this book to learn how to deal with Dicks in other areas of your life, I hope you've gleaned some helpful ideas. If you're married to, working for or entangled with a Dick right now, you have a lot of ideas from Part 1 to help you determine your next steps and find a resolution.

---

11   One, meaning one at a time. There are people who find one, two or even more people in their lifetime to whom they commit and feel a soul connection.

If you're single—consider doing a man-fast. What do you have to lose?

More encounters with Dicks—that's what!

If you feel fairly balanced but just want a little spring-cleaning, try it for 30 days. If you've been seriously dysfunctional in your behavior and choices (if you've called any recent ex a "fucker" or "Dick,"—and especially if you've used the word "hate"—you fit in this category), see if you can go 4 to 6 months.

When you start the fast, you might think that when it ends you'll go crazy and jump on the first offer that comes along for a date or for sex. But you'll be surprised. If you really commit to the man-fast, when you come out of it, you'll be so clear. You'll have such a fresh perspective that you'll ease back into a healthy social life, and your relationships will develop in more balanced ways.

The benefits don't apply just to dating either. You'll find yourself working with better men, sitting next to more courteous men on the airplane, served by more respectful waiters! You'll see change in all aspects of your life—likely with the women in your life, too!

Before you go on your next job interview, before you make a significant change in your life's direction, before you go on one more date…

Do a man-fast.

See if you don't find fun, fantastic friends, great dates or even your life partner and *soul mate*.

Now get out there, be your beautiful self and find all the real wonder that's waiting for you.

Love, Jane!

GIVING BACK

A portion of the proceeds from *Go, Jane!* is donated to:

Patsy Takemoto Mink Education Foundation For Low-Income Women And Children

From the foundation's website:

"As the first woman of color to serve in the United States House of Representatives, Patsy Takemoto Mink's major platform was the concern for women's rights. While she served in the 2nd Congressional District of Hawaii, she established a scholarship program for low-income women survivors of domestic violence.

Every year, five scholarships are awarded to abused and battered mothers who have chosen to take control of their lives and better themselves through education. Recipients of this scholarship may use the funds for tuition and expenses towards a college or technical school of their choosing.

To be eligible to apply, the applicant must have taken her children and left her abusive relationship to find new housing and receive counseling for herself and her children. For more information, visit www.patsyminkfoundation.org."

CONNECT WITH ALLIE CHEE

Website
www.alliechee.com

Blog
www.gojanebook.blogspot.com

ALSO FROM ALLIE CHEE

- If you believe family & friends are your greatest treasures
- If you love caring & cooking for them (or want to learn more)
- If you believe that no matter what income, and no matter what schedule demands—friends, family & community can remain our top priorities...

FREE LOVE was written for you!

Available in print and eBook on **Amazon** and **Barnes & Noble**

PRAISE FOR FREE LOVE

World traveler Allie Chee's new book **Free Love** *is a delight to read with its bits of wisdom, common sense about healthy living, and feeling good about the simple things in life.*

— SCOTT E. MINERS
Editor, *Well Being Journal*

Building true joy means embracing our experiences and using them to create the fabric of our daily joy. In **Free Love**, *Allie shows us how in her uniquely charming and honest way.*

— CHRISTINA PIRELLO
Emmy award winning TV host of "Christina Cooks" and bestselling author

I love **Free love**. *I love that it honestly explores how we make choices, and dares to challenge the ones we are making collectively. I love that it is not preachy, yet inspires deep change in simple, practical ways. I love that it is written from the heart about living from the heart. Definitely a tool for helping us Be The Change that we wanna see!*

— DR. CLAUDIA WELCH, DOM
Author, *Balance Your Hormones, Balance Your Life*

Bring on the free love! This book is a "being while doing" adventure guide through daily life in your own home. And you'll come back to it wanting your moment with Allie Chee and her tales of world travel that spice up every section, because her delightful personality imbues every page and makes you laugh again at the little stuff. Don't get bogged down—get into free love!

— MICHELE RITTERMAN, PHD,
Family Therapist, author, *The Tao of a Woman*

Praise for Free Love

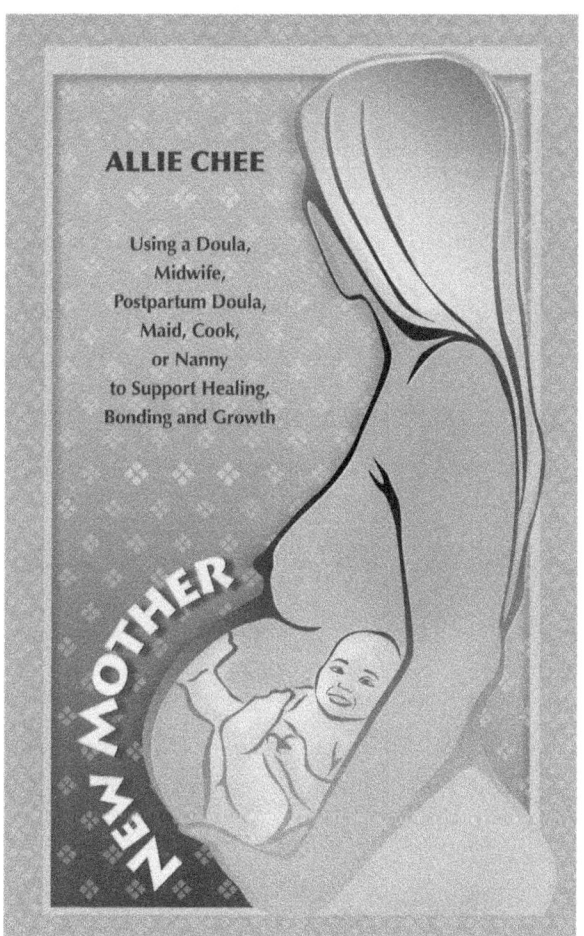

- If you want a natural childbirth
  If you've considered home birth
- If you believe your postpartum time can be magical...

NEW MOTHER was written for you!
Available in print and eBook on **Amazon** and **Barnes & Noble**

PRAISE FOR NEW MOTHER

If you are pregnant or are a new mother you cannot afford not to heed the advice given by Allie Chee in her book, **New Mother,** *if you want to experience the true joy and fulfillment of new motherhood. A very practical book written with humor and wisdom."*

— DR. MAO SHING NI, PH.D., D.O.M., DIPL. ABAAHP

If we're ever going to create a healthy and benevolent world, few things are as important as the way a mother and baby spend their first days and months together. **New Mother** *offers a beautiful vision and practical support for that precious and formative time.*

— JOHN ROBBINS
Author, *No Happy Cows* **and** *Diet for A New America*

I have never read a book like this for new mothers. I think you need it.

— JAY GORDON, MD, FAAP

New Mother *combines practical and helpful information from Eastern and Western practices for pregnancy and postpartum. I will recommend it to my patients and students.*

— DR. NING X. FU, O.M.D., PH.D,
PROFESSOR: FIVE BRANCHES
UNIVERSITY OF TRADITIONAL CHINESE MEDICINE

I cannot wait to share this book with all my patients!

— Dr. Jessica Chen L.Ac., DOAM, Co-author,
Sitting Moon: A Guide to Natural Rejuvenation After Childbirth

www.ingramcontent.com/pod-product-compliance
Lightning Source LLC
LaVergne TN
LVHW041540070426
835507LV00011B/850